A Journey To Self-Peace

By Dr. Abdelfattah Mohsen Badawi

Publications Division
PRASANTHI NILAYAM

SRI SATHYA SAI SADHANA TRUST,
Publications Division
Prasanthi Nilayam - 515 134
Anantapur District, Andhra Pradesh, INDIA
STD: 08555 ISD: 91-8555 Phone: 287375 Fax: 287236
E-mail: orders@sssbpt.org

© **Sri Sathya Sai Sadhana Trust,
Publications Division**

All Rights Reserved

The copyright and the rights of translation in any language are reserved by the Publishers. No part, passage, text or photograph or Artwork of this book should be reproduced, transmitted or utilised, in original language or by translation, in any form or by any means, electronic, mechanical, photo copying, recording or by any information, storage and retrieval system without with the express and prior permission, in writing from the Convener, Sri Sathya Sai Sadhana Trust, Publications Division, Prasanthi Nilayam, Andhra Pradesh India - Pin Code 515134, except for brief passages quoted in book review. This book can be exported from India only by the Publishers - Sri Sathya Sai Sadhana Trust, Publications Division, Prasanthi Nilayam, India.

ISBN: 978-93-5069-089-5

First Edition: July 2014

Published by
The Convener,
Sri Sathya Sai Sadhana Trust, Publications Division
Prasanthi Nilayam, India, Pin Code - 515134
STD : 08555 ISD: 91-8555 Phone: 287375 Fax: 287236

Printed at
Createspace

Sathya Sai's mosque built in 1978
for the Muslim population of Puttaparthi

"Allaho Akbar, La Illaha Ila Allah"

This is the sacred formula of Islam. It signifies that God is the super-most sovereign; Allah is the undisputed, unexcelled Ruler of creation. He, alone, is worthy of worship.

Sai Baba

Dedicated To Bhagawan Sri Sathya Sai Baba

Preface

This book is the thesis of Dr. Abdelfattah Badawi for doctoral degree in comparative religions and mysticism. I found the subject of Sufism and comparative mysticism, with special reference to the Indian mystic Sathya Sai Baba, is well researched and presented. This work will be of immense value for the scholar as well as lay men interested in this area.

Dr. Badawi is a professor emeritus of the famous Egyptian Petroleum Research Institute in Applied Organic Chemistry. He represented Egypt in various international seminars and gave talks at various American universities.

Dr. Badawi is a Muslim, whose scientific reasoning and love for universal love, beyond the boundary of his own religion, naturally lead him to the study of other great world religions in light of Sufism, the mystic part of Islam. Qualified non-dualism of Bhakti Vedanta is the Indian counterpart of the Islamic Sufism and is studied indepth in this work, based on Dr. Badawi's immense interest in Sathya Sai Baba's works. Sathya Sai Baba is a mystic, a philosopher, and a great social reformer of the East.

Dr. Badawi, as an ardent Muslim, has visited Mecca several times in fulfilment of his spiritual obligations and visited Puttaparthi, the abode of Sai Baba, as a part of his journey towards eternal peace, the quest of every Sufi.

This book, in my opinion, is not a negation of the great faith of Islam, but a confirmation of its underlying unity with other great religions of the East. It also clears the doubts of the Western mind on the misconceived fanaticism of Islam. Also, this book is the great homage to Dr. Mohammed Sayed Tantawi, the Imam of Al-Azhar, whose preaching motivated Badawi for the constructive dialogues with other great religions.

For analysing Sufi doctrine, Dr. Badawi combined his scientific logic with the love of Allah, the Almighty, as no logic or scientific reasoning alone can synthesise Islam and Sufism, as the Infinite is far beyond the logic of the finite human mind.

Dr. T.Y. Yousuf
Director, Sufi College,
Hawaii, U.S.A.

Foreword

The author of this book, *A Journey To Self-Peace*, Dr. Abdelfattah Mohsen Badawi, is a member of our Imhotep Scientific Society. I, being the President of this Association, got an opportunity to express a few words concerning his book. He has assembled material from his spiritual journey to attain self-peace, self-realization, and then God-realization, so as to be knowledgeable of God and to achieve the love of God.

The goal of living, whatever it might be, could be pursued and attained more readily, if one acted in accordance with the laws and therefore, realized optimum potential. If one did not do this, he would be poorly prepared to achieve his objectives and would be constantly getting into difficulties.

I was introduced to Sri Sathya Sai Baba's speeches. There are a number of volumes based on these speeches, which clearly show that the purpose of life is spiritual development.

This book is offered in the hope that its contents may be helpful to many readers in their everyday living and thus, prepare them more adequately to continue their spiritual search and development of happiness. I can say it is a perfect guide for those, who are practising self-peace or other exercises to achieve love of God and self-peace; particularly now-a-days, because a human being is moved by matter, instead of making it subservient to him.

He has vast knowledge on self-peace and the exercises of other religions to achieve the righteous path of life. During his spiritual journey to attain self-peace, he met several saints, but he was impressed by Sri Sathya Sai Baba, who teaches his devotees Truth, Righteousness, Peace, Love, and Non-violence to attain self-peace and work for salvation in the midst of their worldly activities.

Dr. Yahya Hamza Koshak, President,
Imhotep Scientific Society,
Cairo - Egypt

Introduction

As a religion, Islam stands for complete submission and obedience to God; Islam means peace, the peace that man establishes with Allah (the Almighty in Islam). Such a person is called Muslim, a word derived from Islam. The meaning of the word 'Muslim' is one, who surrenders to God. A Muslim believes that there is only one God, the Creator, the sovereign Ruler of the living and the non-living in the Universe, with no ascendant and no descendant. A Muslim has a set of well-defined rules to conduct his life, which are known as the five pillars of Islam. They are:

1. Faith in Allah and absolute submission to His will and the messenger of Allah.
2. Prayer, after proper ablution, five times a day.
3. Charity, giving a part of one's income to help the poor.
4. Fasting for the full month of Ramadan, daily from dawn to dusk.
5. Performance of pilgrimage to Mecca at least once in a lifetime, if possible.

Islamic history can be divided into two movements:

Exoteric: From the Prophet Mohammed through the four Khalifas and all the religious leaders.

Esoteric: Spiritual, through the Sufis from 8th to 16th centuries and onward.

Many verses in the Koran suggest that Sufism is inherent in Islam. Zhikr (remembrance of God) was mentioned many times in the Koran, leading man to the spiritual world.

The practice of Sufism with its Zhikr is still relevant and will be able to contribute to the values of the 21st century. Sufism is practised for peace and well-being and Zhikr is therapeutic. Sufism develops the human being as a whole. With this development, man comes to acquire cosmic consciousness.

During his spiritual journey, a Sufi attempts to attain eternal peace. During this journey, he is subjected to Alchemical Transformations, which pruify him from his suspended impurities and thus, liberate him from the forbearing constraints on the Journey of divine love. Along its path, the Sufi reaches self-realization, then God-realization.

I was venturing on the Sufi path, while working as a research chemist over a period of thirty years and I was always accompanied with an enthusiasm and love for Sufism. As a professor of Applied Organic Chemistry and being familiar with the organic synthesis of new compounds, of unique and valuable characteristics, healing and treating illnesses in humans and in the environment, I discovered that Sufism enjoys the same attributes, which are capable of curing human illnesses and relieving man from the sufferings he bears, so that he is alchemically transformed into a pure, cognizant Divine Self.

During my journey on the path of Sufism and the paths in Egypt, which are of the Shazleya and Khalilya doctrines, I discovered myself and I found the Sufi path completely unified with the teachings of two mystics in India, known as the Sai Babas.

The First Sai Baba, known as Shirdi Sai Baba, a Godman (1838-1918) in India, taught the basics of morality and spirituality to mankind through his simple, yet powerful teachings of love, compassion, patience, faith, surrender, equanimity, detachment, and service. He was a simple, illiterate, rural ascetic, Who lived for forty years in an old, isolated mosque at Shirdi, wearing tattered clothes like a Muslim faqir, begging alms and performing all sorts of thrilling miracles to cure, help, and bless His countless devotees and visitors.

The goal of a Sufi aspirant is to reach God-realization - to realize his own inner divinity. Shirdi Sai Baba attained His divine status and throughout His life, He also played the traditional role of a Master guiding others along the path.

Shirdi Sai Baba was observed constantly repeating, "Allah Malik Hai," and it appears that He had a direct experience of Union with

God. He demonstrated God-like powers, such as clairvoyance, the ability to appear in devotees' dreams, or to appear in distant locations. The thrust of Shirdi Sai Baba's whole life was one-pointed, focused entirely upon God, giving up everything for the goal of God-realization. His method was the ascetic, renunciate, mystical path with emphasis on Zhikr, the unbroken recollection of the name of Allah. He is an example of One, Who had achieved the last stages of Sufi attainment, namely Haqiqat, the Truth and Marifat, permanent gnosis as evidenced by His miracles (Karamat). At this stage, annihilation of the separate ego self and of false identification with the body has taken place. This annihilation, termed Fana by the Sufis, is what Sai Baba was referring to, when He said, "This body is just My house." He declared that after His physical death, He would return in eight years, reincarnating in a new body.

The Second Sai Baba known as Sathya Sai Baba was born on the 23rd of November, 1926, in Puttaparthi, as Sathyanarayana Raju. On October 20th, 1940 at age 14, He suddenly threw away His school books and announced to His family and friends that He was Sai Baba of Shirdi, 'His previous body'. No one at Puttaparthi in rural Andhra Pradesh, the birthplace of Sathyanarayana Raju, had ever heard of the saint, Sai Baba of Shirdi, Who had passed away in 1918. Sathya Sai gave many proofs that He was the same Entity reborn. He related numerous incidents and experiences He had as Shirdi Sai.

Bhagawan Sathya Sai's mission does not teach any new cults or religions. He exhorts the individual to become aware of the Divinity that is inherent in him and to conduct himself accordingly, to achieve the ultimate goal of union with the Divine. He calls for human relations that are governed by Sathya (Truth), Dharma (Righteousness), Prema (Love), Shanti (Peace), and Ahimsa (Non-Violence).

He emphasizes devotees of all faiths to practise their own religion by understanding the true spirit behind every religion. He underlines the essential unity of all religions and exhorts all to develop a proper understanding of all religions as being based on love.

Human beings think that happiness exists in their aspirations, which could not be fulfilled. Once their wishes are reached, they realise that they have missed the right path. The fruit that they longed for so long did not give them the pure honey they wanted. Being frustrated, they seek another aim to realise this lost happiness. Life goes on without reaching their aim.

Human beings seek happiness outside their own selves. For this reason, they are lost. Wise men realised, after their long search for truth, that happiness is hidden within themselves and springs out from their own depths.

An American physician once stated that he wrote a list, when he was young, including his worldly requirements, namely health, love, talent, ability, wealth, and fame. He presented this list to a wise man, seeking his opinion. The wise man told him that it is well-designed and in good order. However, he forgot the most important element that cancels all these elements. This factor is written in two words: Self-Peace. This is the gift that God bestows on the chosen people. He grants many people health, money, and fame, however Self-Peace is granted to a few of them. After fifty years of private experimentation, he realised that Self-Peace is the ideal aim of a wise life.

This book presents the meaning of Self-Peace and the means of accomplishing it. It manifests the mercy of Self-Peace on human beings and the human race as a whole.

I present it to the reader, who is my companion in this journey of life, who shares with me the findings of my own experiences, hoping those, who are wise and thoughtful, can benefit from it to accomplish unlimited happiness.

The care I give to the theme of this book is the care given to a baby in his cradle. The reason is my realisation that humanity urgently needs to stop the wheel that rotates without mercy in the whole world. At the threshold of the twenty first century, we need to listen with awareness to the human voice. The human being will become a slave to modern technology, instead of making it a slave for himself. The human being is moved by matter, instead of making it subservient to him. The human being is about to lose his humanity. Materialism has dissolved the human characteristics that differentiate between him and animals. He is ruled by the law of the jungle in a non-ending fight, where existence is for the stronger and not the better. Strength, here, is the ability to devour others and cancel them from the map of existence.

All kinds of weapons are used in destroying civilisation and political weapons are used without any differentiation. This is the law and the concept that rules human beings and the nations of this age. These struggles lead to destruction and toil, loss or gain.

Some nations, today, still keep in their hearts some moral values. However, these morals are in danger to be swept away by the cruel globalisation flux. For this reason, I call upon every human being, who still has some humanity and understanding, to handle the issue of this book with great care, because it aims at happiness for humanity as a whole. If you cannot help others to accomplish inner peace, at least do it for yourself and extend it to your family.

All religions agree in worshipping God and calling for ideals, high moral standards, and seeking Self-Peace. All these morals cannot be attained without achieving spiritual principles based on truth, charity, love, and wisdom, which provide one's self with peace, satisfaction, optimism, and health.

Sai Baba explains these principles, which identify the road to Self-Peace and guarantee the true happiness of man, springing from his true inner self. It also saves his self from the dangers of globalisation and its purely material concepts. The road to true peace starts with complete faith in God, pure love of human beings, overcoming desires, instincts, and whims of the human self.

It is important to know the self through spiritual discipline, confidence, patience, persistence for righteousness, virtuous deeds, and high morals (the basis of the world).

To walk the path of God requires continuously remembering His Holy Name and merging in His Holy Love, developing love in the heart and great care for peace of mind. This is followed by silence, solitude, seeking the Holy Light, and listening to the Holy Voice. How graceful is peace, in remembering the name of God with a pure heart, deep loyalty, and complete truth! How graceful are the light spots opened in the heart, when contemplating God!

The end of this road is great and delightful, when the human being feels the love of God for him and when his soul is overwhelmed with tranquility. His conscious remains alert, revealing the light of God inside himself. The person pursues peace, forgiveness, surrender to God, and serving people, content with what he is offered.

The human being will find health in optimism, joy, and peace. These are the most magnificent instruments for remedy of the soul. He will realise the bond between health and nutrition qualitatively. He will understand the strength of faith and good deeds as the way of healing and freeing the mind from anxiety, hatred, prejudice, and greed. My book reveals the ways and means for fulfilling peace inside the human soul, the highest creation of God. We ask you to read it more than once. Please accept my deepest greetings and may peace be bestowed upon you.

Contents

Preface..vii
Foreword..ix

CHAPTERS

Introduction..xi
1. War And Peace Within Man...1
2. Spiritual Alchemy..7
3. The Divine Alchemy..19
4. Sai Baba And Sufism...27
5. Truth Is One..33
6. Righteousness And Good Character................................39
7. Seek Peace In Faith And Surrender.................................47
8. Loving Allah...59
9. Serve All...69
10. Non-Violence..77
11. Health In Happiness And Peace.....................................83
12. The Self-Peace Path...97
13. Divine Discourse Of Bhagawan Sri Sathya Sai Baba
    On 1st January, 2001...113

APPENDICES

Appendix [A] Passage To India...121
Appendix [B] From Paris To Brindavan............................125
Appendix [C] A Journey To Sai Baba. The Interview.......129
Appendix [D] A Journey To Self-Peace............................131
Symptoms Of Self-Peace...147
Bibliography..149

Chapter - 1
War And Peace Within Man

"Man's mind is responsible for both his slavery and freedom, so that if he dominates his senses, he should be on the way to his freedom and vice versa. If man doesn't dominate his senses, he will convert to a slave of his desires, which shall not abandon or leave him in peace till his death."

Sai Baba

Since the creation of the human being, man has been living in hardship and toil, for since the very day of his birth, he has been suffering life's hardships, whose joys are blended with pains and what people suffer of abuse by hand and sharp tongue. It was mentioned in the Glorious Koran:

"We have created man in endurement." [Al-Balad - 4]

Then comes man's egotism and his disrespect of others, his attempt to dominate others, anger, violation of human rights, greed, and love of possession - all this inflicts upon its owner tension, violence, and hostility, both on the individual and communal levels. Thence arises crises, conflicts, and wars between mankind. Alfred Nobel considered that every man is infested with a germ, whose content ratio varies from one person to the other, such germs being exemplified in personal battles, envy, and gossips.

Man's Crisis

Man is indeed in perpetual crises with his desires and blood boiling eroticism, which he strenuously seeks to fulfil during his short lifetime. Man wants wealth, position, authority, and sex. He is in a perpetual state of emergency and turmoil. Man never quenches his thirst or satisfies his hunger, as Prophet Mohammed said:

> *"Should man be allotted a valley of gold, he would appeal for a second and should he be given the second, he would still appeal for the third, and nothing would fill up man's belly other than dust."*
> *[Al-Bukhari]*

There is, moreover, another crisis, which confronts man outside himself, from which there is no escape, such as the death of a dear person, illness of one of the family members, marital disagreements, work related problems, or a change in the financial situation, and such external factors, which augment the acuteness of the tension within man. It is a war, whose field is man's body and its impact determines his health. A battle, which revolves around evil and virtue, a conflict between immorality and chastity, egotism and excitation, lie and truth, hatred and love, harm and non-violence, revenge and conciliation, contention and worship, atrociousness and devoutness - it is a war and a duel between the self aligning with evil and the assured self, so that if the evil aligning self is victorious, the body endeavours to destroy itself with psychiatric and nervous illnesses, such as anxiety, tension, and depression or organic diseases, such as high blood pressure, heart diseases, diabetes, rheumatism, intestinal ulcer, colon inflammation, or malignant diseases such as cancer. However, if the assured self is victorious in this war, man enjoys health, happiness, self-restitution, and peace.

Sai Baba, the social reformer from India, ascertains that tension and anxiety in modern life and the distortion in the whole environment destroys man's health, and He warns that there is an increase in the numbers of people, who suffer from corporal ailments and psychiatric illnesses all over the world; and since the creation of man, he is in a perpetual state of suffering and always being haunted with a feeling of fear and tension. Man, meanwhile, feels a yearning to come back to his Creator, God, where there is peace, calmness, and security.

Tension Victims

During the twentieth century, science and technology advanced tremendously and it was supposed that they would render life more peaceful for people; but, actually, this advancement primarily resulted in multiplying the acuteness of tension and stress in daily life.

For, along with the progress of the standard of living came increased pollution, unemployment, violence, and terrorism, and we began to find it difficult to find an equilibrium and peace within ourselves. This results in our falling victim to tension and consequently, family dissociation, misunderstandings rising acutely, divorce rates increasing, and accidents increasing.

Our lack of peace and security as a result of daily life pressures relatively influence our psychological and corporal health. The most dangerous illnesses and influences bearing upon our health are high blood pressure, arteriosclerosis, and cardiac cringes, which result in more than 50% of the yearly deaths on the global level. Such illnesses have crept into the younger youth and the scientific interpretation for that could be an inadequate diet, lack of motion, and heritage tendency and another factor, which we always neglect, namely tension and lack of internal peace, thus the negative impact of this on the heart's intactness.

Many times, when man is inflicted with tension, doctors prescribe him sedatives and when man suffers corporeal symptoms, he vists an internal medicine doctor. Pressures of life in our modern age and our lack of feeling of inner peace lead to a rise in blood pressure, which is widespread today and will further spread during the coming years.

When we confront a tension filled situation calling for a change in our attitude, a spontaneous response takes place, causing a rise in blood pressure, an increase in the heart pulse, and a speed up in the rate of respiration, so that blood flushes to the muscles, urging us to either fight, or escape. This reaction is found in animals and is that, which is termed 'fight or flight response'.

Tension is considered one of the subjects, which have acquired the special concern of psychiatry and physiology. For, there is emotional tension arising from family disagreements or resulting from the death of a beloved person. There is an environmental tension, such as exposure to excessive temperatures and there is a physiological tension, resulting from an over-hormone excretion in the adrenal glands. The adrenal hormone is viral, excreted by these glands for the survival of the living organism in case of their exposure to danger.

Psychologists, in the college of Medicine at Washington University, subdivided the events to which man is exposed and which lead to tension. They tabulated them in a table, titled 'Degree of Social Compatibility Tension Scale', which was set up according to personal interviews with 394 samples. Doctors found that widowers and widows are apt to early death and it was found that for persons after divorce, the ratio of illness rises. Doctors deem that any change towards the better or worse are from the factors causing tension to mankind.

Doctor Walter Canon, professor of Physiology at Harvard University, described the case of 'fight or flight' as a phenomenon resulting from tension, which has prevailed towards the end of the twentieth century as 'contingent reaction', orienting man to run or combat and repetition of this phenomenon leads to a chronic state, converting temporary rise in blood pressure into a continuous one.

Realising Inner Peace

The question here is whether there is a means to cure tension and convert the state of war within our bodies to a state of peace and restitution during our daily life. Is it possible to limit the risks of rise in blood pressure? The answer here is found in the inner peace of our minds, which is only realised through truth, righteousness, loving God, serving others, and non-violence.

These principles, if we apply them to our daily lives, render us victorious in the wars within ourselves, give us peace in our hearts, and give us inner reassurance and self-restitution, consequently leading to a state of relaxation in our muscles and reductions in our unconscious nervous system's activity, thus making high blood pressure return to its normal state.

In times of hardships and catastrophes, man becomes aware of his need of inner security and peace. Peace is the gem, which enriches our life. A life, upon which peace resides, is that life of the reassured self, which has been awarded and dedicated in adoration and love. Peace augments self-immunity and provides it with protection against psychological shocks from external effects. Peace dawns in the soul and the person's liaison with God becomes firm and effective.

With the growth of peace within the self, man naturally shares this peace with others and gradually, universal peace is obtained for a better world.

Man's paradise is his inner world, in which he can enjoy peace and which is a state of rest of mind, free from tension or anxiety, and whoever finds this peace has no fear in his heart, no matter what the challenges are.

Inner peace comes from the dominance of the higher self; that is to say, man being endowed with the attributes of the higher self - faith, love, truthfulness, virtuous work, non-violence, lack of vanity, and service of others.

Inner Peace

Sai Baba deems that inner peace for man is only realised by abandoning worldly desires. The search for peace does not necessitate migrating to another place, for as gold and silver are hidden under the ground, pearls and emeralds are lying under the sea, so is peace and happiness lying hidden within the depths of our minds and we only have to dive within to be able to find them.

Sai Baba assures the necessity of our reliance on God's blessing, so that we do not contract illness and that we place our confidence in

God, rather than in medicine. And instead of resorting to drugs and tonics, we should seek help in prayers, God's remembrance, and exulting Him, for in them are vitamins we need, which preserve us. There is no healing medicine but God. Hospitals are only allocated for those, who have faith in medicine and doctors.

Man, who enjoys inner peace, speaks words of love and truth, and abandons anger and greed; whereas man, who yearns for position, wealth, and shameful desires, is exposed to pressures and tension, and does not enjoy peace of mind and is apt to illness.

Chapter - 2
Spiritual Alchemy

"They do not know that God can give such men not only merely food, but Amrith (Divine Nectar)! The Name of God is enough; It has all the potentiality needed."

Sai Baba

Amrith in ancient Sanskrit refers to the secretion of the pineal gland, following the yogic metaphor, even as a tiny drop of this nectar may, under proper conditions, influence all the glands and chakras, and confer enlightenment.

Spiritual alchemy has been used to describe spiritual practices from ancient Egypt and elsewhere, which lead to transformation and realisation, in which all apparent opposites - masculine and feminine, heaven and earth, divine and human, the whole and the part, the visible and the invisible - body, heart, mind, and spirit are reconciled, integrated, and made whole. The underlying principles of the universal human concept are the same as those that guide the evolution and development of the universe and life itself. The core alchemical maxim as above reveals what we learn about the atom, teaches us about the solar system and what see in natural processes around us, and reveals the pattern of our own inner development. Edgar Cayce explained in reading (137-181) that every physical being is composed of atomic force and each atom is a universe in itself, with a mind of its own, under the supervision and influence of the body's mental faculties.

The process of spiritual transformation is a part of the Great Work, which is at the same time a spiritual realisation. This fact is very often overlooked in alchemical studies, claiming alchemy to be wholly a spiritual discipline (Sadhana).

In order to obtain the *Elixir*, man has first to triumph over obstacles, which culminate in the production of the *Philosopher's Stone*, which has the property of transforming base metal into gold.

The Sufi Mystic Path

Only through reliance on inspired intution, the light replaces darkness and limitations of the mind are transcended by the Avatars (Godmen) and the great masters.

Once, we decided to follow the sufi or mystic path, use our free-will to love Allah, and become ready, the master appears and we truly are born again. We are changed forever, alchemically. We will never be the same, once the transformation process begins. This is the path of spiritual alchemy. The best authority on spiritual alchemy is our inner guidance and our awareness that when we meet our master, God is the force listening. As soon as we see the master, we will steer ourselves toward inner peace, put our light on the map that shows our unfolding path, and attract God's grace by allowing our inner self to reflect *Divine Peace*. The journey to inner peace takes time, patience, persistence, and faith. After we have gone within and transformed our lead to gold, we will naturally attain the real peace just by direct and constant awareness of God.

In Alchemy The Secret Art, Stanislas. Klossowski de Rola reports that the Emerald Tablet has been always highly considered by all alchemists of all centuries. They make constant reference to it, such as, "As Above, So Below." It confirms the analogy between the macrocosm and the microcosm. The further one grows in the knowledge of the principles of alchemy, the richer one becomes in inner-standing. Then, one will be tempted to dismiss the whole thing as did Jabir, the Arab Alchemist. If the student is patient and humble enough, the first intuitive sparks igniting in his spirit will encourage him to continue, until he begins to separate the true from the false.

The theory of the four elements (Earth, Water, Air, Fire) were syncretized at Alexandria and finally, developed by the Arab alchemist,

Jabir, Razi, and Ibn Sina. All science was imbued to mysticism. It was told that the mind embraces everything and that all that exists is nothing but the mind, which contains bodies of all kinds. This remarkable statement (which is echoed in mysticism) is the corner stone, upon which rests the edifice of magical alchemy, the purpose of which is to attain a realisation of the perfect archetype of the absolute.

Elixir Of Life

The Foundation of mysticism teaches symbolically the fundamental unity of all substances and their inherent faculty of transformation. To the alchemist, the faculty of transformation has a universal meaning. This miraculous power of transformation went far beyond the ***Philosopher's Stone***, which is supposed to fulfil all wishes or the ***Elixir Of Life***, which guaranteed an unlimited prolongation of earthly life. He, who experiences this transformation, has no more desires and the prolongation of earthly life has no more importance for him, who already lives in the deathless. That Elixir gained by the way of miraculous powers loses in the moment of attainment all interest for the seeker, because he has grown beyond the worldly aims, which made the attainment of powers desirable. In this case, the means sanctify it into a higher aim.

Titus Burchardt, in his book, 'An Introduction To Sufi Doctrine', describes that the different natural qualities of the soul are combined in different states. Equilibrium of the soul consists of a steady alteration of expansion and contraction, comparable to breathing, and in a marriage of the fixed activity of the spirit with the liquid receptivity of the soul. In order that it may be possible for this synthesis to take place, the powers of the soul must not let themselves be determined in any way by impulses coming from outside. They must instead respond to the spiritual activity centred on the heart. Here, the pre-eminent spiritual means of sufism is the verbal symbol either aloud, or inwardly, with the synchronising of the breath; hence, the various phases of the inner alchemy.

The Divine Name

During dhikr (invocation) of the name of God, the doctrine of truth, virtue in the will and spiritual alchemy are summed up in a single inner act; virtue is the human reflection of the divine aspect, symbolised by the sacred Name, while the spiritual alchemy will result, in its most intimate working, from the theurgic power of that same Name, which is mysteriously identical with God. Here, the will suddenly unveils the centre of consciousness, so that renunciation results. A sacrifice may, in certain cases, bring with it, suddenly, the vision of the eye of the heart. As for spiritual alchemy, this transmutes the pyschophysical structure of man into radiation of Grace, which is mysteriously present in the divine Name. The objective of dhikr, with performance of a series of movements in unison, is to produce a state of ritual ecstasy and to accelerate the contact of the Sufi's mind with the cosmic mind, of which he considers himself to be a part. Here, the movements develop the body, the thought focuses the mind, and the sound fuses the two and orients them toward a consciousness of divine contact, which is called Hal (condition). Sufi dhikr (invocation) has been explained by Al-Ghazali in a passage that has been summarised by D.B. Macdonald and cited in 'A Moslem Seeker After God' as follows:

Let the worshipper reduce his heart to a state, in which the existence of anything and its non-existence are the same to him. Then, let him sit alone in some corner, limiting his religious duties to what is absolutely necessary, and not occupying himself either with reciting the Koran, or considering its meaning, or with books of religious traditions, or with anything of the sort. And let him see to it that nothing save God the most High enters his mind. Then, as he sits in solitude, let him not cease saying continuously with his tongue, "Allah, Allah," keeping his thought on it. At last, he will reach a state when the motion of his tongue will cease and it will seem as though the word flowed from it. Let him persevere in this, until all trace of motion is removed from his tongue and he finds his heart persevering in the thought. Let him still persevere, until the form of the word, its letters and shape, is removed from his heart and there remains the idea alone, as though clinging to his heart, inseparable from it. So far, all is dependent on his will and choice; but, to bring the mercy of God does not stand in his will or choice. He has now laid himself bare to the breathings of that mercy and nothing remains, but to wait on what God will open to him, as God has done in this manner for prophets and saints. If he follows the above course, he may be sure that the light of the Real will shine out in his heart.

The Heavenly Wine

The more the sufi listens to the divine Name, the more his consciousness becomes free from all the limitations of life. The soul then floats above the physical and mental planes without any special effort on man's part, which shows its calm and peaceful state. A dreamy look comes into his eyes and his countenance becomes radiant.

He experiences the unearthly joy and rapture of ecstasy. When ecstasy overwhelms him, he is neither conscious of the physical existence, nor of the mental. This is the Heavenly wine, to which all sufi poets refer and is totally unlike the momentary intoxication of this mortal plane. A heavenly bliss then springs in the heart of the sufi, his mind is purified from sin, his body from all impurities, his spirit is ***alchemically transformed***, and a pathway is opened for him toward the worlds unseen. He begins to receive inspirations, intuitions, impressions, and revelations. He is no longer dependent upon a book or a teacher, for divine wisdom, the light of his soul begins to shine upon him. Here, the ego bound, narrow human personality effaces itself to make room for a higher state of Being to transcend the limitations, imposed by the senses, to be in a position to grasp the hitherto intangible, and to know the previously Unknowable. When the contact takes place, it has the effect of divine intoxication so beautifully expressed by the sufi poets. In this state of ***sat-chit-ananda*** (existence, consciousness, bliss), the enraptured soul, breaking the restraining bonds of the ego, loses all idea of the body, the world, and the objects of the senses in the contemplation of a surpassingly blissful, intensely alive, and extremely fascinating state of being, which human language completely fails to portray.

Without a living *Master*, spiritual alchemy wanes, as a lamp goes out, when the oil is exhausted. The real *Master* always teaches man that God is within him, he always shows his devotees the exact way to God realisation, and helps them to Self-realisation. For this very important reason, a living *Master* is always essential.

The Greatest Miracle Of Sai Baba

The greatest miracle of the living Avatar (Godman) and Universal Master Sathya Sai Baba is the *Power To Transform*. It takes ages even to bring about an iota of change in a person's attitude and vision, in spite of being close to him. But, Sai Baba can transfix and bring about a complete metamorphosis in the human personality through a mere smile, a word, or a gesture. That is the most significant sign of Divine Alchemy. His most extraordinary feat is that He apparently leads one of the most important simple lives lived by any person, but boredom never seems to afflict Him. On the contrary, He performs the same actions of walking amidst His devotees, receiving their letters, speaking a word of solace each time, with renewed enthusiasm and joy. Each Darshan (looking at the Master) is unique. He is an *Ocean Of Love*, a wish-fulfilling tree for His devotees, the very *Avatar Of Love*, the Voice of one's own innermost heart speaking to each individual externally, a Promoter of the unity of world religions and a philosophy that embraces Matter and Spirit.

God Realization

Sai Baba says that until realisation of God, the name of God can be used; the idea of separation will end only with merger, not before that. One has not to waver or doubt, once the person is convinced as to the effectiveness of this method.

Sai Baba stresses that there is no need to retire into a forest or cave to know your inner Reality and to conquer your lower nature. Win the battle of life by being in the world, but free from attachments.

Man is steeped in illusion and he cannot free himself from this illusion. He forgets his origin and he does not understand the Universal Absolute. However, if this situation did not exist, there is no reason why the overself should come as an Avatar (Godman) at all. What exists as a reality is only one, but what we see is manifold. What is real is the Supreme-Light. This ***Supreme-Light*** is the splendour of the Self. That has been called the ***Light Of Oneness***. This light of oneness, as Sai Baba says, is the ***Light Of The Self***, which is the embodiment of Bliss. You can only experience the embodiment of Bliss and it is not possible to exhibit it in any other manner. You are the image of the ***Supreme Self***, the image that is reflected in the body that is part of Nature. It is to discover, in and through this agitated world, the ***Peace*** that is your birth-right and utilise that peace of the illumination of the heart, which will reveal the splendour of the Self which you really are. Sai Baba assures that the devotee must so act, so that the heart of the guru melts at his devotion. Only that will cleanse the mind of evil and vice. If man develops devotion and steady faith, he will achieve the glory of ***Self-Realization***.

Equal Mindedness (Samadhi)

In every spiritual practice, the object kept before the mind being either God, or Self, or the Guru, prescribed for meditation, complete absorption of mind in the object plainly signifies ***spiritual alchemical transformation*** in the interior of the sufi mystic. This denotes the development of a new quality in his consciousness, which, assuming the image of the Master, keeps the attention of the seeker from wandering and holds it completely engrossed in contemplation, in the same way that a magnet holds a piece of iron tightly attached to it by the sheer force of attraction. Here, the state of union with God (fana in Sufism) is attained and samadhi is experienced, when the mental flux becomes entirely restricted and the stream of thought becomes one with the Master contemplated. The ceaselessly repeated expression *Sat-Chit-Ananda*, meaning *Existence-Consciousness-Bliss*, is symbolic of the enrapturing Trans-human state of consciousness experienced in samadhi bliss.

Sai Baba says that when it is realised that the knower is *Pure consciousness*, the act of knowing is *Pure consciousness*, and that, which is known, is *Pure consciousness*, there is then no more agitation or mental activity. This is samadhi. Samadhi is as the ocean to which all spiritual discipline flows. Every trace of name and form disappear in that ocean. One will not be aware that he is experiencing. There will only be *Oneness* and nothing else. That will be samadhi, which is nothing except *Pure consciousness*.

The Vital Spiritual Energy (Kundalini)

The mystical experience is an incomprehensible phenomenon of consciousness. The flash of divine intoxication may last only a few moments, or it may continue for an hour, or several hours, or even days at a time. Shams-i-Tabriz, the Sufi poet of Persia, experienced the state of union with God and was in a state of divine intoxication. *"In a place even beyond outer space, in a tract without a trace of shadow, soul and body transcending, I live in the soul of my loved One anew,"* he says.

Kundalini is divine in nature and has the same unlimited powers as are associated with God (Allah) by the Sufi-minded. With such a conception of the divine energy (Kundalini), it is no wonder that the ancient Sufi mystics have exhausted the power of their devotion in investing kundalini with all the powers - Omnipresence, Omnipotence, Omniscience.

According to Sai Baba, in order to awaken kundalini and make it rise to the Ajna chakra (eyebrow centre or the third eye), the person has to concentrate on this chakra. He has to sharpen his concentration to a very fine degree and shut out all other sensation, feelings, thoughts, and emotions. Meditation as described by Sai Baba is the royal road, the easy path for awakening kundalini and in order to be effective, there must be steady practice with no hurry and no worry. With steady practice, the person will become quiet and the state of meditation will naturally come about. Call upon God. He will help you. He will respond and He Himself will be your guru. He will guide you. He will always be at your side. Think God, see God, hear God, eat God, drink God, love God. That is the easy path, the royal road to your goal of breaking ignorance, which is one with God, Sai Baba says.

Kundalini is able to destroy, when awakened, the evil tendencies inside the mind; so be dedicated by all for the propitiation of the outer as well as the inner divinity, in order that the outer and the inner worlds may have *Peace* and *Joy*. By means of systematic sadhana (spiritual practice), it is possible to tap the inner resources that God has endowed man with and elevate yourselves to the purer and happier realm of the reality.

The Spiritual Energy Centres (Chakras)

The sufis define *'Spiritual Growth'* as the development of a latent intuitive capacity present in all human beings, where the sufi becomes aware of the subtler, deeper currents that reflect and permeate reality. When this takes place, the sufi experiences his continuity and identity with God (Allah). At some stages, the Sufi asks himself the question, "Who am I?", "Which powers work through me?", and, "How can I realise my full potential for *Love* and *Peace*?" *"I am He, Whom I love; He, Whom I love, is me,"* says Hallaj.

As the mystic journey progresses, the orbs of light (chakras) grow. Their growth refers to the inner ascent through seven strata, called *Latifa*. There is homology of function between Latifa and the chakras, which are the centres of consciousness and the organs of supersensory perception. The seven esoteric meanings of the Heavens in the Koran exactly correspond to the structure of a mystical physiology, seven subtle organs or centres (Latifa). The first centre is the ***acquired*** subtle body (qualab), the second centre corresponds to the soul, the centre of uncontrolled desires (nafs ammara), the third centre is that of the personal individuality (ana), the fourth centre is related to the 'secret' or superconsciousness (sirr).

The fifth centre is the spirit (ruh), the sixth centre is related to the Latin term arcanum (Khafi), and the seventh centre is related to the divine centre of being, the eternal seal of the person (haqqiya).

The sufi would need a master to lead him to the degree that is in truth the divine centre of his being (haqqiya), where his higher spiritual ego opens.

According to the Sufi Najm Kobra, the Sufi seeker is called the 'particle of light' imprisoned in darkness and Kobra declared that his own method was none other than of ***alchemy***. This alchemical operation is what produces the aptitude for visionary apperception of the suprasensory worlds, these being manifested by the constellations, which shine in the skies of the soul. These spiritual constellations are exemplifying on the master (Imam), who is the pole, just as in the term of ***spirituality***, ***alchemy*** is the ***'Elixir'***.

According to Sai Baba, the first lowest chakra is the embodiment of the nature, the second chakra at the point of the navel is the guardian of the sphere of five senses and is the fire principle, the third chakra the next higher is the water principle, the fourth chakra is the region of the heart and it embodies the air principle, the sixth chakra on the mid-brow spot is the embodiment of the splendour of Awareness, for when this chakra is reached, man glimpses the Truth, gets ***transformed***, and becomes translucent; only a step away from the final realisation, when the seventh chakra on the crown of the head is attained.

Sai Baba says that the stage of awareness is most evident in the sixth and seventh chakras, where the awareness is latent in everyone, ready to surface when the veils of ignorance are removed. The individual life-force resides like a lightning flash, in the womb of a blue cloud. It will be alert and awake, only when the spiritual practice of any type is done after the cleansing of character and habits.

Spiritual Transformation

The Sufi looks at the soul as having different modes of existence. Seyyed Nasr, in 'Sufi Essays', reports that as for the doctrinal aspects of Sufi psychology, the human soul is then presented as a substance that possesses different faculties and modes of existence, separated yet united by a single axis that transverses all the modes and planes. A state like patience is a virtue, which means that when the soul reaches such a state, not only does it possess the virtue in question, but its very substance is *transformed* by it, so that during that stage of the way, in a sense, it is itself that virtue. In Essence: The Diamond Approach to Inner Realization, Almaas describes the concept of stations as stages of inner development in Sufi methodology. This development is seen as a *transformation* of essential substance from one aspect to another, until they are all realized. Essential *transformation* is, in other words, transubstantiation.

Baba says that transformation (alchemy) has to take place in the minds of men. Right thoughts will lead to right actions. That is why scriptures have declared that the mind is the cause of man's bondage or liberation. Mere world practices or instruction cannot help man to achieve Divine Consciousness. It can be done only by spiritual discipline, for it is a basic transformation.

Sai Baba asks, "What are the social evils?" His answer is that they are accusing others continuously, blaming others, making fun of others, and feeling jealous. We have lost peace in society, because of these bad qualities in man.

Baba advises men to develop divine feelings at all times. Therefore, we have to foster good qualities in society. We have to foster qualities of helping others. To do service, we should develop sacrifice. We should have the spirit of equanimity, a feeling that other's suffering is our own suffering. Then, there will be a spiritual change, compassion, mercy, love, forbearance, sympathy, such noble qualities originate in *Spiritual Transformation*.

Sai Baba says that if men, today, suffer from restlessness and lack of peace, their own actions are responsible for this state. He advises men to make their thoughts pure. Realise that they are human and that there is the Divine in the human. Man has the option to pursue the external (worldly objects) or seek the bliss that is eternal. By their good thoughts and good deeds, men can transform the state of the nation.

Chapter - 3
The Divine Alchemy

"Love is the only Alchemy, the only solution in Kali Yuga. It is the only possible weapon with which to fight the evil tendencies."

Sai Baba

The Divine alchemy transmutes human clay into something noble and indestructible, that makes from a base substance a precious spiritual distillation.

Love is the path, the love of the person for his Creator, the individual for the Divine, the man for God. Only in this way does inner alchemy of Divine love transmute the entire existence into a Divine fire with a Divine purpose.

Whereas chemistry deals with scientifically variable phenomena, the alchemy constitutes the hidden ESSENCE of all religions. Alchemy teaches the latent forms of things **(TRUE ESSENCE)**, according to their truth and not according to their appearance.

If consciousness is transmuted from an ordinary (lead like) level to a subtle (gold like) level of perception, the **TRUE ESSENCE** can be realised as the highest love.

There are precise links, fundamental to alchemical thoughts, between the visible and the invisible, above and below, matter and spirit. Gold, because of its incorruptible nature, is to the alchemist the sum of matter, an analogy of the ultimate perfection, which they themselves seek to attain by helping these base metals to reach the blessed state of gold.

True alchemists have actively sought the universal Medicine, which, ultimately sublimated, becomes the Elixir Of Life, the Fountain

Of Youth, and the key to Immortality in a spiritual and physical sense. This Elixir rejuvenates the human body into an incorruptible **'BODY OF LIGHT'**.

The Adept (he, who has attained the Gift of God) would then be crowned with the triple crown of Enlightenment, Omniscience, Omnipotence, and the joy of Divine Eternal Love. But, the very few among the few have succeeded in reaching the ultimate goal.

The gold-making is relatively of little consequence comparable to the super-power obtained by the great Sufis, which are important by-products of high spiritual attainment.

The Roots Of Alchemy

The roots of alchemy are derived from the Egyptian endeavour to create an eternal body. Many procedures are actual continuations of the Egyptian's chemical attempts to mummify the body for the continuation of spirit and soul after death.

In the seventh and eighth centuries, there was a flourishing period in Arabic countries, after which alchemy evolved with the history of chemistry. According to Ibn Sina, the famous Arabic philosopher, if a person in a state of meditation and inner exaltation can approach the creative power of the Godhead, then if he, in that stage, violently desires something, it appears in the outer world as a miracle. Ibn Sina calls this 'ecstatic contact' with the creative power of Godhead. Ibn Sina confirms through the gift of prophecy that through certain techniques of ecstasy reached by long exercises of meditation, the soul of man acquires some of God's power. It is on that assumption that Alchemical Activity and Transformation are based. Anyone, who does with repetition experimental prayers, meditations of Devotion and Love, changes his own personality and acquires divine power, by which he will succeed in producing Alchemical Transformation.

God is the highest and greatest that nobody can conquer. Divine Love has a great inner value. This inner value is the greatest treasure. It is loving to everybody and hostile to no one. "Change yourself," the heavenly wisdom says, "from a dead Philosophical Stone into living Philosophical Stone." Within one's Self, but not from his ego, is everything, which he needs and which he wrongly seeks outside. The light, which we must find within us, belongs to God, Who has put it into us. So, the truth is not be looked for in our ego, but in God, Who dwells within us. There is no God, except God and in Him is the whole of existence.

By finding the ***inner truth*** within ourselves, all doubts get slowly dissolved. In the ***alchemical*** sense, it is the melting of our false egos and putting them into an inner melting pot, out of which comes the one ***inner truth***. We have to begin with ourselves.

In Sufism, alchemy is sometimes used to describe the practice of dhikr (invocation). The soul in its chaotic, unregenerate state is lead. The Philosopher's Stone is the Divine Name, in contact with which the soul in lead is transmuted into gold, which is its true nature. This true nature is revealed unveiled and realized by the practice of dhikr. The alchemical work thus symbolized ***spiritual realization***. The essential work is a transformation of that, which is base, into that, which is noble. Thus, the macrocosm (the outward soul) analogically coincides with the microcosm (the inner world, or soul). Of all spiritual practices, the dhikr is the practice most apt to free spiritual energy, that is to allow the particle of ***divine light***, which is in the Sufi, to rejoin its like. According to the Sufi Najmoddin Kobra, the dhikr sinks down into the well of the heart and at the same time, lifts the Sufi up out of the darkness of the well. Here, alchemy involves extracting the subtle organism of light from beneath the mountain, under which it lies imprisoned.

Silent Invocation

Complementary to dhikr is the constant silent invocation of the Divine Name at all times of the day and in the midst of other activities. Naqshbandi Sufis are known as the 'Silent Sufis', because they practise the silent meditation of the heart. In the Naqshabandi tradition, the dhikr is practised in silence. The silent dhikr produces in the heart an intense and imperishable impression (naqsh = 'impression, print'; band = 'to bind, to fasten'). There are no set of times or places for practice of remembrance. Allah, the Beloved, is remembered always and everywhere, either individually, or in groups. Through the practice of dhikr, the seeker revives the latent memory of the primordial state of utmost nearness to the Beloved as God and experiences the Oneness of Being. The Naqshbandi devotees believe that their life is a journey to the Beloved and that this journey is not possible without a guide teacher, who has surrendered totally to the will of Allah. They believe that ultimately, the outer teacher points to the inner teacher, who resides in the depths of all men and women, and that all paths lead to Allah.

The Arabic language beautifully brought out that, "God and His Name are one." Thus, from Dhakara (to invoke) is derived from Madhkur and Dhikr (invocation). According to Sufi doctrine, it is God Himself Who invokes, God Himself Who is invoked, and God Himself Who is the invocation. This Divine Act should pass through man for salvation. Madhkur-Dhakir-Dhikr corresponds to the Hindu ternary Sat-Chit-Ananda. Sat is the Divine object, Chit is the Divine subject, and Ananda is Divine Union. Sat-Chit-Ananda, often translated as 'Being-Consciousness-Bliss', hence object-subject-union.

The Egyptian Sufi

According to Ibn Ata Allah, the great Egyptian Sufi, silent invocation begins with the heart with effort, then comes invocation with the heart, and then comes possession of the heart by the invoked and effacement of the invoker. This is the secret of Prophet Mohammed's saying,

> *"Hidden remembrance is seventy-fold better than remembrance, which the guardian angels hear."*

The sign of the invocation's reaching the innermost self is the absence of the invoker from both invocation and the invoked. The invocation of the Self is ecstasy and drawing in it. Prophet Mohammed also said,

> *"A people do not sit invoking God without the angels surrounding them, mercy enveloping them, peace descending upon them, and God remembering them amongst those with Him."*
>
> **Prophet Mohammed was asked, "What type of worship is best and most highly esteemed by God on the day of judgement?" He said, "Invoking God Most High."**

A man said to Prophet Mohammed, "Verily, the religious laws of Islam are numerous and I have become old. So, tell me something, which I can follow, but do not make it too long for me, lest I forget." The Prophet said,

> *"Your tongue should not cease to be moist with the remembrance of God."*

The Prophet's wife, A'ishah, said that Mohammed the Prophet used to remember God at all times.

> *According to Koran, God said,*
>
> *"And he, whose sight is dim to the remembrance of the Beneficent, we assign unto him a devil, who becometh his comrade and lo! They surely turn from the way of God and yet, they deem that they are rightly guided." (43:36-7)*

According to the Sufi Ibn Ata Allah, Al-Hamid Al-Aswad was with his master Ibrahim Al-Khawass on a journey and they came to a place, where there were many snakes. He unsaddled his mount and sat down, so Al-Aswad did like that. When the night began to cool and the air to chill, the snakes came out. Al-Aswad cried out to this master, but he said, "Remember God!" So he did and the snakes left. Then, they returned and Al-Aswad called out to his master, but he said the same thing. Al-Aswad did not cease being in that state till morning. When they arose in the morning, the master got up and walked, and Al-Aswad walked with him. Suddenly, a huge snake, which had been coiled around his master, fell from the inner folds of his garment. Al-Aswad said to him, "Did you feel it?" The master answered, "No, it has been a long time, since I have seen a night more pleasant than last night."

The Name Of God

According to Sai Baba, of all various spiritual practices, repetition of the name of God (Dhikr) is the most effective. Just the repetition of the name of God is of no value, but if the repetition is chanted with full knowledge of its significance, it has great effect. Sai Baba assures us that God will answer to the Name, for which the aspirant thirsts, provided the yearning comes spontaneously from a full heart, a pure heart. It is the feeling in the heart that is the crucial test, not the length of time.

Sai Baba says that the rosary is very useful for beginners in spiritual practice, but as you progress, Japa (invocation) must become the breath of your life and so, rotation of the beads becomes a superfluous and cumbersome exercise, in which you have no interest. When you have no worry about your duties or shopping, do more invocation. Do it with love and enthusiasm. It should become natural with you to do so. There is no need for rosary or sitting in meditation, while your mind is preoccupied with worldly matters. The invocation you have to perform is constantly to remind yourself of the Divine within you. Win the battle of life by being in the world, but free from attachment.

Sai Baba says that the Lord's name is like a mountain of sugar. So long as the sugar is on the tongue, you feel the sweetness in taste. Similarly, so long as the heart has love, peace, and devotion, you feel bliss.

Knowing the meaning of one's life from one second to another is immortality, the state in which we constantly enjoy the presence of God.

According to Sai Baba, immortality is the meaning of liberation. Liberation is when you have lasting *joy* and lasting *peace*.

Considering the inner truth of God's presence within ourselves, we taste it again and again. From day to day, there will come sparks before the inner mental eyes and slowly, these sparks coalesce into a light that, in time, one will always know what one needs and will thus, only be attached to that *inner truth* (Allah), by which great tranquility and great inner peace of mind are acquired by constant awareness of the self. Then, you slowly become aware of the presence and reality of the self. That gives the ego *peace of mind*.

Chapter - 4
Sai Baba And Sufism

"He, who has not seen the pathway to Allah, remains blind in the world - then, he wanders like a blind among people."

Shirdi Sai Baba

"One cannot be happy without the peace of mind that is got by pure devotion."

Sathya Sai Baba

The recent discovery of a manuscript of a notebook, written in Urdu by Abdul, Shirdi Sai Baba's pupil, has helped to confirm Sai Baba's familiarity with Sufism. The thrust of Sai Baba's whole life was one-pointed, focussed entirely upon God-realisation; His method being the ascetic, renunciate Sufi path, with emphasis on dhikr, the unbroken recollection of the name of God. He constantly repeated the Name, "Allah Malik Hai."

The Perfect Master

According to the Sufis, there must always exist upon the Earth a man, who is a perfect channel of Grace from God to man and is given the title Qutb, which means 'Pole of the Universe', a realised **Perfect Master**. According to some Sufi authorities, there can only be one Qutb on the Earth at any one time. Sai Baba was obviously aware of His universal role, although He never referred to it directly.

It is, therefore, appropriate to refer to Sai Baba as the Universal Sufi Master, for by His own admission, He achieved the state of divine **Union with God**. He came to bridge the Hindu-Muslim gap, according to His famous saying,

"Ram (God of Hindus) and Rahim (God of Mohammedans) are one and the same."

The Main Sufi Stations

In view of Sufism, if we analyse Sai Baba of Shirdi, we shall see that His method was characterised by **Three Main Sufi Stations**: Poverty, Patience, and Surrender. The fourth station of the Sufi path is Poverty. Sai Baba always identified Himself as a faqir. He did so in a spirit of humility, emphasising His nullity before Allah, "What am I? A petty faqir! I am not God. How great is God! No one can compare with Him."

Moreover, it is known that divine intuition can only be received, when the Sufi keeps himself hungry and empty. Fasting is therefore a key technique, the 'alchemy of hunger', an empty stomach being a requisite for enlightenment. Sai Baba taught moderation in diet, which is really wholesome both to the body and mind.

Patience is the fifth station of Sufi path. Among the characteristics of a faqir, *patience* is perhaps the most important one. Sai Baba said about this station that, one can realise God via patience. Patience has been mentioned almost one hundred times in the holy Koran. It shows the greatness of the patience station and it is the master of all virtues.

Surrender to the divine (tawakkul) is the sixth station along the Sufi path and is perhaps the most important. Once a Sufi has entered the highest surrender, he is naturally brought to the condition of satisfaction (rida), in which he opens himself to the states of divine grace. Prophet Mohammed said, ***"You, poor people, give God heartly satisfaction, you will win."***

We reach a conclusion that the main Sufi stations on the life of Shirdi Sai Baba were *poverty, patience, and surrender* to God. Above all, *Devotion* came at the introduction, body, and conclusion in Sai Baba's message.

Like the Shirdi master, Sathya Sai Baba propounds the Universal message of devotion and love of God, which is the core of both Sufism and Bhakti and the essence of all religions. Thus, He demonstrates that the identity of the two Sais is the same, although appearing totally dissimilar.

Sathya And Poverty

Prophet Mohammed visited a poor man to find he owned nothing, saying,

> *"If the light of this man is distributed on the people of Earth, it will be sufficient for him."*

The prophet also said,

> *"Poverty of a believer is better than a good saddle on a horse's back."*

If we analyse Sathya's view of poverty, we find that He says,

> *"It is unknown and very difficult for the rich to live with the poor, to take on the problems and sufferings of the poor. But, this is what I'm telling you to do. Go to the poor, live with the poor, be with the poor, the helpless, the suffering, and serve them."*

As a gesture of His compassion and love towards the unfortunate of the earthquake in Gujarat, Sri Sathya Sai Baba despatched 33 lorry loads of articles of daily need for distribution, on 8th February, 2001. The material was well-packed quantity-wise and handed to the householders in a cordial way, with love. The work of distribution of material in every affected household, in about 108 villages, required working day and night and covering thousands of miles in vehicles, on roads which were not good.

Sathya And Patience

Patience is one of the ranks of the masters of attitude in Sufism, who have patience on abuse and on abating whims, who, when visited by pure souls, endow them with perpetual security and peace in the abode of blessings. It was said in the glorious Koran,

> *"Peace rest upon you for what you have been patient, blessed be the outcome of the eternal abode."*
>
> *(Al Ra'ad-24)*

Sathya Sai advocates that the virtue of patience is the most important virtue and among all good virtues, with which man can be trimmed, patience and clemency occupy the topmost position.

Sathya assures that the virtues of mercy, sympathy, and patience are these, which distinguish man from animal. There is no virtue excelling patience. Patience is equivalent to truth itself.

> **Whatever obstacle is encountered, whatever troubles and problems arise, a man with a resolute nature remains firmly committed to pursuing the tasks, which he has undertaken, until he achieves his final goal. If you do not have the quality of determination, then patience will have no basis and cannot develop in strength. Patience and determination are twins; one cannot exist without the other. Without determination, patience cannot establish itself and without patience, determination will degenerate into arrogance.**

Sathya And Surrender

Surrender means loss of ego or individual identity. When a seeker comes to God to pray to Him, he is supposed to have surrendered himself totally. A man can be stable in surrender, when he becomes humble and serves everyone with sincerity and humility.

The grace of the master is essential for spiritual peace. Without the grace of the master, a seeker cannot progress, not even a step; and books do not contain grace. Only a living guru can grant that. The grace cannot be earned without accepting the guru. Sathya says that, the guru helps us to cross this ocean of worldly sorrows and troubles, if we surrender to him wholeheartedly and fully.

> *Sathya asks, what is meant by surrender? Forgetting the body and thinking of God, that is surrender. Surrender to God and to life means being of the same nature as God. But, such a state is beyond man's will. Surrender is when doer, deed, and object are all God. It cannot be forced. It comes naturally to a heart filled with love for God. God is as a spring of fresh and sweet water in the heart. The best tool, to dig a well to that inexhaustible source and savour its sweetness, is the repetition of the name of the Lord. Dedicate every action to the Lord and there will be no place for ego. This is the quickest way for the ego to subside.*

Sathya And Devotion

Sathya Sai Baba says that, all education, all wealth, all ritualistic worship or penances, all are of no value without genuine devotion to God. He mentions that God can be worshipped in many ways. His name can be repeated, His glories chanted, His true nature contemplated in meditation. Devotion directed to the Lord is called Divine Love and is the easiest of all paths for the realisation of the goal.

> *Recognising and being established in the feeling that the Lord of All is the One, Who is resident in all hearts, that is the sacred path. Devotion should be the unified expression of Love of God, action in the service of God, and total surrender to the will of God. Devotion, Worship, and Awareness of the self together demonstrates the Oneness of the Divine.*

> *Devotion is a fragment of the divine. Without divine, awareness of the divine cannot be experienced. The true mark*

of devotion is the pure love of God. Without this pure love, bhajans, worship, and the like are artificial experiences and are valueless.

One should regard love of God as the greatest treasure one can have. When you love God, you will have love towards all, because the Divine is in everyone. Therefore, bear in mind: *Love all; Serve all.*

Today, people carry on routine reading of scriptural texts. This serves no purpose, unless they lead pure and sacred lives. They should fill their hearts with the love of God and share that love with others.

True devotion means getting rid of vices of attainment, hatred, and envy and manifesting pure love. The devotee has to overcome hatred, envy, and attachment and experience the *peace* and *bliss* of love. That devotee will then acquire all the attributes of the Divine.

Devotion has been defined as desireless love for the Lord. Any prayer to God for fulfillment of a desire cannot be called devotion. God should be loved for His own sake. Love should be fostered for its own sake. True devotion is a combination of selfless service and love. *Devotion to the Divine will give you Bliss, and Prosperity, and Peace.*

Chapter - 5
Truth Is One

True Islam guides man to concentrate on the One, the Only wholly, so that truthfulness will be realised by God. Peace is an inner feeling with truthfulness at its foundation.

Sai Baba

Truthfulness for the Sufi Imam Abu Bakr Al Razi is one of the heart stations in Sufism. Truthfulness is the truth; it is one of God's names in Koran,

> *"Praise be on His greatness the Truth King, no God but Him, generous God of the throne."* **(23:116)**

The truthfulness is His creation and what He contained of knowledge into the universe as in Koran,

> *"Have you not seen that God created truthfully the skies and the earth."* **(14:19)**

All people acknowledge and believe in the existence of God, but most of them pray, go to mosques, read Koran fast, and perform Al Zakat and Haj. However, they do not find inner peace, because they are not truthful or sincere in what they do. They practise worship automatically without soul, or selfishly, to gain temporary benefits, acting as merchants, with their worshipping devoid of truthfulness.

Truthfulness with self and with God requires us to worship God as if we see Him, truthfully and sincerely. The more honest one is now with God, the more peace he feels, as God gives His honest worshippers safety, comfort, and tranquility.

Man will not have peace, until he listens to the voice of truth inside and concentrates on the One only nearer to him than his cord of life, until he unifies finally with the truth experienced by Al Ghazali, Ibn Arabi, Jalal Al-Din Al-Rumy, and other big Sufist figures.

The Prophet Mohammed said, *"Search truth, even if you see destruction in it, as it is the real safe way."*

Ahmed Ibn Khadwaih also said, "He, who wants God with him, for him truth is a must. God is with truthful people."

Holding Onto Truth

Al Sheikh Al Ghazali says, "God has truthfully created the skies and the earth and asked people to go on living truthfully, to say only and to do only what is truth. The perplexity of people is due to their estrangement from this truth basis, to their surrender to lies and illusions towards themselves and their thoughts that have taken them away from the straight forward path. Therefore, it is a pivotal support in the Moslem's character to hold onto truth in everything, as the Holy Koran says, *"You faithful worshippers, fear God and say truth sayings. Then, God will fix truth your work for you, forgive you your misbehaviour."* (**Al Ahzab - 70-71**)

During direction of man to the truth and his spiritual journey, man is assimilated with everything but truth and feels nothing in existence but truth, and his action and will, as is said in the Holy Koran, *"You see their eyes full of tears of the truth they have known."* (**Al Mae'da - 83**)

"We will show them our signs in the universe and in themselves, so that they will know it is the truth." (**Fouselat - 53**)

Sufi Experience And Truth

Ibn Arabi thinks that through Sufi experience, man realises his self unity with truth. The truth is an absolute truthfulness that appears in his manifestation in the universe. Divine manifestation in man and the eternal process aims at knowing truth, with the appearance of his means and character on existence, as in the divine saying, *"I had been a hidden treasure and liked to be known. I created people, then they knew me."* On the level of observing truth in the Sufi heart, the ending vanishes in the endless and he sees God alone, and He is known to him by taste, as in the Holy Koran,

> *"For the knowledgeable to know it is the truth from your God."* **(Haj 54)**

> *"And we truthfully created them, but most of them do not know."* **(Al Dokhan 19)**

Man is always looking for peace, but cannot find it, except within himself. When man realises this truth within himself, he will see it everywhere. The target of man's life is to be honest and with the truth, as is said in the Holy Koran,

> *"Say may our God get us together and judge truthfully, He is the knowledgeable One to make the truth decision."*

The Eye Of Absolute Faith

When man concentrates his efforts on the truth and it is called upon, that truth cleans up hearing and sight from contamination with materialism, until man reaches the level of tranquil self and starts the journey to the key of satisfaction and peace, and the eye of absolute faith opens up and he sees clearly the truthfulness, as the Holy Koran says,

> *"And worship your God, until you have absolute faith."* **(Al Hegr - 99)**

If man is bestowed absolute faith and gets to see things with the eye of absolute faith (which is insight or the third eye), his mind acquires the knowledge of absolute faith that is reserved only for good God-followers, as in the Koran,

"We uncovered your cover and your sight is as strong as iron." **(50:15)**

The eye of absolute faith is strengthened only by God-fearing, purifying the heart by truth. Then, it sees a lot of God-songs that make man more faithful and peaceful. Absolute faith is a light thrown by God on the hearts of prophets, God-worshippers, and God-followers, according to their merits, and it tops the level of satisfaction. The prophet used to get up at night and worship God, saying,

"Praise be upon You, You are the truth, Your promise is truth, so is Your encounter, Your heaven, Your hell. Prophets are truth, Mohammed is truth, and the day of reckoning is truth."

Truth Is The Basis Of The Universe

Sai Baba points out that God manifests in truth and truth is the basis of the universe, the truth remains and does not change with time, man has to live honestly and to realise that God is in everything, and when man knows the truth inside himself, which is the essence of his nature, he will understand his truthfulness.

Truth does not simply mean refrain from lying, but for man to make truth his true essence and the spring of his life, and to give up everything for truth. The world appeared shining in fear from truth and keeping away from truth. In the absence of truth, man will fear to live. Truth carries security for man, truth protects the whole world and makes it move, truth stops fear. When man secures truth, he will not be afraid and will recognise God. For man to be divine, he has to let the truth, good manners, and fine attitude be the basis of his life. Lying destroys humanity, so that man has to speak out truthfulness without fear and regardless of any consequences. As important as the foundation is for a house and the roots for a tree, so is the truth important for man's life.

Sai Baba assures that hesitation in truth does not make for safety or security in man's life Truth and good work are like man's two eyes or the bird's two wings, mutually dependent things. The whole universe has come out of the truth and to truth it shall return. Truth is God, God the wise and the merciful. Truth does not end. It is God, the eternal. Man has to follow truth. Man himself is the law of truth and good work. All powers martial, moral, military, or political give in to the truth and good work. Victory is always for truth and good work.

Each one has a trait of truth; he cannot live without it. Each man has love and light. Without it, life becomes a dark vacuum. This light is God, the source of truth, love, and mercy. Man searches for love to give and share; his nature is love and mercy.

God Is The True Love Itself

Waves do not separate from the sea. Heat and light cannot separate from the sun. So is love. It is inseparable from truth. They are forever together. Truth without love is a light that burns; love without the truth is a disturbing dream. The great love should be for truth.

Man's nature is to look for love and truth, from which springs his soul. They are the basic sources, from which man acquires his spiritual survival. Man came from God and to Him he shall return. In this changing world, it is that light that leads man home. This light is the truth, good manners, good behaviour, self-control, non-attachment, forgiveness, and non-aggression, which man is deemed to possess.

Chapter - 6
Righteousness And Good Character

"Islam teaches the human being that Divine Happiness may only be achieved by Virtuous Deeds, not by wealth, learning, or power."

Sai Baba

Righteous deeds are fear of God in all our acts. It is the first Sufi station for all virtuous human beings, who fear God, according to Abu Bakr Al-Razi. God the Almighty said in Koran,

"The most distinguished for God are those, who are more fearful!" (**Al-Hograt - 13**)

Abu Saeed Al-Khudri said that man came to the Prophet Mohammed, saying, "Oh messenger of God, advise me." He answered, *"You must fear God, this embraces all virtues. You have to fight for God and this is nunnery for the Moslems, and you have to remember God, Who is the light for you."*

Those, who do righteousness, live in tranquility of soul and inner peace with themselves. In many verses of the Holy Koran, we find that faith is related to righteousness more than sixty times. Some of these read,

"Those, who are faithful and do virtuous deeds, are the owners of heaven and will live forever." (**Al-Bakara - 82**)

Every righteous deed, no matter how small it is, will be greatly prized. The Messenger of God said, "Do not disdain any good deed, no matter how small it is, even if it is a smile for your brother."

God prepares for those, who do righteousness, a great reward, which is far above their imagination. God the Almighty said, "The soul does not know the great reward hidden for it, for what it has done." The holy saying reads,

"I have prepared for My virtuous worshippers what they had never seen or heard or thought of."
(Al-Bukhari)

The Moslem scientists explain righteousness as worshipping God and dealing with others at the same time. The main cause of the declining of Moslems was their differentiation between worshipping and dealing with others.

Sheikh Mohammed Al-Ghazali says that Moslems paid heavily, when they retired from the daily life fields and thought that religion was only words or celebrations.

The Voice Of Conscience

Every human being hears an inner voice springing from his heart. This voice speaks to him and guides him to do good deeds and stops him from non-virtuous ones. This is the voice of the conscience, which is honourable and speaks to the person to do virtuous deeds. Behind the conscience is a force protected from any wrong - the force of God, the Peace. All of what is far from God is evil. All wrong doings towards your brothers are evil. No peace or tranquility may be present with evil deeds.

Virtuous deeds mean that a person does what he thinks is right, no matter how many difficulties he faces, challenges sources of evil, and stops them. He overcomes the animal instincts hidden within himself. He works hard to develop his soul and ascends, until good deeds become an essential part of his nature. At that point, the person reaches the circle of peace.

Righteousness And Conscience

Sai Baba says that righteousness is what a person does with purity of thought, word, and act. The nature of the human being makes his behaviour in tune with his thoughts, words, and acts. When there is a contradiction between thought, word, and act, the mind becomes void.

How could a person know at any situation if his act is virtuous or not? All that causes no harm to the person or others is a virtuous deed. Another measure for the righteousness is to do what you say and to say what you feel, not to falsify truth or contradict your conscience.

Sai Baba says that some people have bad thoughts, hear bad thoughts, see bad acts, and spread scandals. They have no righteousness and no peace. People must have loftiness in their lives, springing from their Godly nature. They must not descend to the level of animals.

Today, every step of the human being takes him away from virtuous deeds. The thoughts of the human being are full of evil. His desires are selfish. The religious and disciplinary struggles spread widely and narrow concepts flourish. How can we call any person a human being, if he has no conformity in thought, word, and act? Where are the virtuous deeds? They are present in your thoughts, words, and acts. Virtuous deeds live in the hearts of human beings.

To do virtuous deeds is to live according to your conscience. To act without conscience is wrong in itself. The love of God in your acts is righteousness. To love God in your speech is the truth. Truth in thought is peace. Purity of heart is the best guarantee for obtaining peace.

Sai Baba Says On Character

"If there is righteousness in the heart,
There will be beauty in the character.
If there is beauty in the character,

There will be harmony in the home.
When there is harmony in the home,
There will be order in the nation.
When there is order in the nation,
There will be peace in the World."

Character for the Sufi Abu Bakr Al-Razi is the highest degree of the heart. In the Holy Koran,

"You are of great character." (**Al-Kalam - 4**)

The character is the image of the spirit and the heart. God, with His great wisdom, gave every human being his character and nature.

Morals And Islam

The most important factor affecting peace and human civilisation are morals, which control the world and bind human beings. The problems of the world, today, are ruled by hatred, grudges, terrorism, wars, and bloodshed. These could not be resolved, except by high moral values.

Moral values are the most important factors that helped in building the Islamic civilisation in the past. The desertion of these morals lead to the deterioration of this civilisation.

Islam pointed strongly to good characters and called for developing them in human beings. The man is considered religious, according to his high morals.

God ordered His Messenger to have high morals, "Push strongly for the best morals. You will find your enemy as your best friend." God ordered His Messenger, saying, "Fear God, wherever you are. Follow evil with good deeds to cancel it and treat people with good manners." The Messenger of God also said, "The faithful, who have complete faith, are those, who have the best manners."

The essence of Islam is represented in the human moral values, for which is sent to us His Messenger Mohammed to ensure it, as he said in his honourable sayings, *"I was sent to complete high morals."*

It was mentioned by Al-Ghazali that a bedouin asked the Prophet Mohammed to define for him the religion. He answered, *"It is high manners."* The Messenger of God always asked his Creator, saying, *"I ask you for health, vitality, and good manners."*

Good manners are based on love, mercy, and forgiveness. God put these characteristics in the human container, so that the human society may live in peace. These characteristics lead to spiritual harmony between the heart and the mind and offer the human being inner peace.

Manners Come Before Worshipping

Imam Mohammed Al-Ghazali, who passed away, proved that manners come before worshipping in Islam. He saw that the cause of humiliation of Moslems, today, is their desertion of the essence of their great religion. Our true disaster is our manners. He said that, the religion of a person is never complete, unless he conforms to the manners and high moral character of the righteous religion. He mentioned what God the Almighty said in the Koran,

> *"I send My messengers, bringers of good tidings and warners. Those, who are faithful and virtuous, will have no fear or grief."* **(Al-Anaam - 48)**

The Imam Al-Ghazali spoke about the degree of manners in the Islamic belief, where he found that manners come before worshipping. He depended on the saying of the messenger, that, "A person is a hypocrite, if he is a liar, not trustworthy, and does not conform to his promises, even if he prays and fasts." The second points to, "Three men, who are the fuel of hell, the reader of Koran, the charitable with his own money, and the fighter for God, if his acts are done for hypocrisy's sake."

Good manners in Islam comes first, followed by worship celebrations of prayers. Worship is the complementary factor. It only gives the outer attitude. Islam is not a form of religious celebration. It is a religion of love, mercy, truth, virtue, honourable manners, and peace.

Imam Al-Ghazali says that without purity of heart, worshipping becomes only speeches and images. At the end, it is a witness that the Moslem man knew the right thing, but did not do it. He read, but did not understand. He saw, but did not comprehend. The great Islamic Preacher says that you see the man praying, putting his hands on his breast while standing and putting them again in this position, after rising from kneeling, making a fuss about it. If you speak to him about a matter for the welfare of the nation, he disappears at once.

The West And Crisis Of Morals

The Western civilisation allowed the human being to realise his instincts and neglect morals and ideals. It strengthens his animal instincts and ruined his inner peace. Mahatma Gandhi considers that the Western civilisation may be suitable for them, but is a disaster for the Easterners. The Westerners must change their concepts about life in order not to reach extinction. Their ambitions for material wealth made them slaves and polluted their souls, which led to their coming generations.

The Western civilisation is today, at a most critical point of restlessness. Western thinkers admit this clearly. It is facing dangerous challenges of deviation, fragmentation, and destruction of the soul, mind, and character. This leads the person to losing his inner peace. We should not sacrifice the human soul for the sake of material progress. We must preserve our moral and religious standards. These are the values upon which the Islamic society was built, through its beliefs, worshipping, and social life. Without those values, we can never attain the inner Peace for the human being.

The Decline Of Moral Values

Sai Baba assures us that moral values result from righteousness. Moral values among people, today, are declining continuously. Good deeds, moral values, and spiritual matters are continuously decomposing and that is a dangerous omen. Bonds were cut among people, due to ideological and religious differences among the educated and the thinkers. Thinkers, who call for these differences, are increasing quickly, while those calling for unity are declining. Behind these struggles, one truth is clear - that humanity is not able to desert its animal nature.

To change the world from this existing situation, we don't need a new social regime or a new discipline. It is necessary to form groups of men and women having high moral thoughts. The presence of these groups will offer the world the Godly light. To form these groups, it is necessary to have a strong base of morals and good deeds. These cannot be obtained without spiritualism. Any great society must be built on a spiritual basis, based on purity, moral values, and good deeds.

Everything in nature is subject to laws and rules. Human beings alone broke the laws of existence. Animals follow their instincts. They have certain seasons for reproducing. The human being does not follow his organising rules. He must be taught the rules of good behaviour and morals. The only way to be taught is the spiritual root. Without spiritualism, the human being will never discover the light inside him.

The decline of moral values caused distortion of human beings, today. Technologies reached great horizons, today, and caused great changes. The most important of these changes is the destruction of morals and values. The generations, today, must be well aware of high morals more than knowledge. The progress of society may never be attained without men having high moral base.

Finally, Sai Baba expresses His sorrow for the absence of morals and good deeds. Money is the only thing people count as important and seek to increase it. However, money and all that it gives does not achieve peace. Peace can only be found by discovering the Divine light within each one of us.

Chapter - 7
Seek Peace In Faith And Surrender

"Islam means surrender or peace. The inner meaning of this term is that man should surrender to God and live in peace with his fellow men."

Sai Baba

A British orientalist, named Khaled, has spoken about peace and Islam. He explained the implications of the Muslim greeting, when it is uttered by every Muslim, who lifts his hand to his forehead and puts it down to his chest, as if he is saying to the person saluted, "To you I give my mind, when I lift my hand in salutation and to you I give my heart, when I lay my hand upon my chest."

The word 'Islam' is derived from the word peace or *'Al-Salam'* in Arabic. Islam is the religion of love, cooperation, tranquillity, and fraternity. The word 'peace' means submission and quietude. Hence, Islam is the religion of submission to the free-will of God. The Holy Koran refers to the word 'peace' in over 80 verses, each with a different meaning:

"The faithful servants of the Beneficent are those, who walk upon the Earth modestly and when the foolish ones address them, answer, 'Peace'."
(The Criterion - 63)

The Muslim seals his prayer with a greeting of peace to God, "Sincere greetings, salutations, and prayers to God. May the peace, mercy, and blessings of God be upon their Prophet. May peace be upon us and upon the obedient servants of God." By this greeting, a Muslim concludes his prayer, turning his head to the right and to the left.

Peace in Islam means security and tranquillity for man as referred in the following verses of the Holy Koran:

> *"It was said (unto him): O Noah! Go thou down with <u>peace</u> from us and blessings upon thee."* **(Hud - 48)**

> *"<u>Peace</u> be upon you, because ye persevered."*
> **(Thunder - 24)**

> *"Peace on him the day he was born, and the day he dieth, and the day he shall be raised alive."*
> **(Mary - 15)**

> *"We bring thee a token from the Lord. And <u>peace</u> will be for him, who followeth the right guidance."*
> **(Taha - 47)**

> *"Praise be to God and <u>peace</u> be upon His slaves, whom He has chosen."* **(The Ant - 59)**

> *"O fire, be coolness and <u>peace</u> for Abraham."*
> **(The Prophets - 69)**

> *"But, when ye enter houses, salute one another with a greeting from God, blessed and pleasant."*
> **(The Light - 61)**

> *"And there greeting therein will be <u>peace</u>."* **(Jonah - 11)**

> *"The word from a merciful Lord (for them) is: <u>peace</u>!"*
> **(Ya sin - 57)**

The word 'peace' is derived from one of the Divine names of God (Al-Salam). There is also the general linguistic meaning of peace, which is security, tranquillity, love, harmony, tolerance, and mercy.

Islam exhorts mankind to opt for peace. The word 'Islam' is derived from submission to God. This submission brings forth peace within the human soul, quietude of heart, and lucidity of spirit. Therefore, God's greeting was that of peace.

> *"Their salutation on the day, when they shall meet Him, will be: <u>peace</u>. And He hath prepared for them a goodly recompense."* (The Clans - 44)

> *"Those, whom the angels cause to die (when they are) good. They say: <u>peace</u> be unto you! Enter the Garden, because of what ye used to do."* (The Bee - 32)

> *"(Nought) but the saying: <u>Peace</u>, (and again) <u>peace</u>."* (The Event - 26)

In the Hadith, Prophet Mohammed (peace be upon him) said, "Spread the word of <u>peace</u>, pray thee when people are asleep and ye shall enter paradise in <u>peace</u>." Prophet Mohammed has made spreading the word of peace one of the signs of love. In another Hadith, Prophet Mohammed said, "Would you like me to guide you to what you live?" They said, "Yes, Prophet of God." He answered, "Spread the word of <u>peace</u> amongst yourselves."

The Quest For The Sanctuary Of Peace

We have to seek peace earnestly and sincerely. It is that peace of the quiet and natural soul. The kind of peace that awakens our spirits and opens our eyes to our true spiritual existence, rendering us in a state that enables us to find a place, where we can take refuge within ourselves when overwhelmed by the battles of life. This place would be the sanctuary and safe haven, where we can seek refuge from the boisterous storms of life to discover an indescribable peace beyond the confines of the mind. Only then can we see the naked truth of the world and realise that it is nothing, but a transient illusion.

Although the strains of life have forced us into the heat of the battlefield, we are there physically, but not spiritually. Our body is in the battlefield, yet our soul is hovering above in peace and tranquillity as described by our Prophet Mohammed (peace be upon him), when he said in the Hadith, "Be as an alien or a wayfarer in this world."

Let us set up a sanctuary within ourselves, where quietude prevails as a haven for our souls in case they grew weary under the stress of cumbersome burdens. Let us find the kind of peace sought by each pilgrim in his prayer, upon entering the house of God in Mecca, from the door of peace:

"God, our Almighty Lord, You are the source of all peace, greet us with peace and let us enter paradise, the house of peace. Exultant and glorified is Your name."

The Peace Within Man

Many people try to find peace in their families, workplace, or in their country, wherever they are in the world. Many of them have been seeking peace through the ages. However, peace is forever elusive and few are those, who have been able to attain it and even if peace is realised, it is just glimpses of a momentary sense of tranquillity.

Finding eternal peace in this life may seem an impossibility. Attaining this kind of peace requires the human feelings to undergo a metamorphosis. This entails steering the soul away from the relentless pursuit of social nature or wealth towards the heart, the abode of the soul.

In Search Of The Supreme Being

Prophets and apostles have recounted their experiences of contact with God in the scriptures. They have spoken of the heaven above, where one can find the fountainhead of peace and eternal happiness beyond the boundaries of time and peace.

Man can live in harmony with his inner self, if he calibrates his thoughts and feelings towards God. Only then can the eternal and meaningful peace be realised. In this connection, Sai Baba emphasises that it is only the thought of God, which can bring about peace, the more mundane thoughts vanish and the more divine thoughts will blossom.

No doubt the mind tends to drift to worldly thoughts all the time, but when we interrupt the sequence of such thoughts, peace prevails. This is exactly what total peace is all about. It is the kind of peace, which results from the absence of desire, anger, greed, and hatred.

Faith In God

"Faith in God, Who is present everywhere, is the key to tranquillity and peace."

Sai Baba

Faith in God for the Sufi Al-Kashiri is the discipline of soulness.

"The faithful is the name of God, the peace, the faithful, the protector." **(Al-Hasr - 23)**

Notice here that peace comes first and is followed by the faithful.

God puts tranquillity and peace in the hearts of those, who have faith in Him. Their belief increases. God alone owns the soldiers of earth and heaven. He manages them as He wishes. He knows everything. His wisdom is the greatest, capable of administrating everything in the Whole World.

It is mentioned in His Holy Koran,

"He descended peace in the hearts of the faithful to increase their faith and their faith in God. God owns the soldiers of earth and heaven. God is knowing and wise." **(Al-Fath - 4)**

Faith in God makes the person fearless and bestows on his soul security and peace, concerning worldly blessings in life with all its unjustness and tyranny.

Faith in God keeps the person in continuous peace. He does not fear death, because it is for the faithful an outbreak from the prison of the body and a transfer from one phase to another and from one home to another. Jalal Al-Din Al-Rumi said, "The tree does not yield its fruits, unless the flowers bloom and fall down. Similarly, the soul does not find or be strong or wear new clothes, unless the body is rotten and the person puts off his rotten life."

A virtuous man felt, on his knees, that the end was very near. He washed his body and perfumed it. He prayed to God. When they entered, he was dead, facing the Kiblah. At his head, they found a paper, where he wrote the following poem.

"Tell my brothers when they saw me dead...

They bewailed and lamented me sadly.
Do you think that I am your dead man...

In the name of God, this corpse is not mine.
This is my image and this is my body.

It was my garment for so long.
I am a bird and this is my cage.
I flew out to freedom and it stayed empty.
Thank God for freeing me...

And building me a home in the highness.
Don't think that death is non-existence.
It is only a transfer from here to there."

Faith in God deepens the inner peace of the soul and helps the person heal from the diseases of the body, mind, and soul. The loyal, deep faith is an effective instrument for overcoming anxiety and restlessness of the soul. Many phenomena prove that daily reading of the Holy Koran gives the person warmth and tranquillity, and helps him cure many of his pains.

Devotion Is The Nutrition Of The Soul

Most patients are not in need of medical treatment. Their diseases are not in their bodies, but in their thoughts and sentiments. The main ailment in many diseases is the great distance between them and their religion. Sixty percent of patients are non-balanced mentally and spiritually. Devotion is the nutrition of the soul and without it, the normal body pains.

There is a close bond between faith and healing. Patients, who have strong faith in God, heal more quickly than others.

Patients suffering from diabetes have their own griefs and desperations. They burn a great amount of energy through these sentiments and utilise a great amount of insulin, secreted by the pancreas, until it is ailing. If the person realises his sentimental life and abides in religion and in a strong faith in God, he will fulfill inner peace, which protects him from the germs of fear and virus of grief.

> *The sign of faith in God is clear in the words of the Almighty, "Those, who are faithful, are more loving to God."*
>
> **(Al-Bakara - 165)**

The Messenger of God put the condition of faith to be the love of God. The almighty Abou Zeid, Al-Akeily said, "Messenger of God, what is faith?" He answered, *"To love God and His Messenger more than any other."*

Sai Baba And Faith

In our path of the Love of God, faith is revealed and becomes the cornerstone of peace. Sai Baba assures us that if our faith in God is deep and strong, we will have no fears when we are sure that our God, Whom we worship, is everywhere in every living thing and in everything. If we lack this strong faith in God, we will experience fear every moment and every step. We will have these fears in exams, when we travel, when we wake up in the morning, and even if we are in bed, we will be afraid of thieves breaking into our homes and stealing our possessions. We will have our fears everywhere and all times. Faith in the existence of God everywhere is the key to peace and tranquillity.

Faith is necessary for the progress of humanity in all fields. Faith is strength and without it, life is nearly impossible. The main basis of peace is faith, love, devotion, and renunciation. Without faith, worship has no meaning.

Today, the wife has no faith in her husband and similarly, he has no faith in her. Children doubt their parents and parents are suspicious of their children. Students have no faith in their teachers and teachers doubt their students. How can then faith flourish in the field of Religion?

If faith is complete and strong, the blessings of God, the Almighty, comes instantly and completely. The person may fulfill this complete faith by worshipping God. Hundred percent of faith comes forth from the soul. Faith is strong and complete even with pain and grief.

While the person suffers from his spiritual journey, he must be certain that God is his best Protector. Anxiety vanishes through faith in God. The faithful person can overcome all obstacles more than the unfaithful.

Be faithful in God and His blessings. Seek for gaining these blessings, using your intelligence and sentiments that God bestowed on you.

One hundred percent of Divine Love is fulfilled by one hundred percent confidence in God and one hundred percent faith in Him.

The highest rank of Divine Love is fulfilled when the person is mentally bonded to God, where he feels security and tranquillity.

Your faith in God provides you with complete confidence in Him. You must have confidence that God's blessings are always with you and that God is your Protector. You must believe that God will never fail you, that He is at your side, helping and strengthening you through your difficulties.

The worst stupidity is to lose your faith in God, when you lose the one you love. No one is born or lives for another person. Everyone is responsible for his sins. Don't let any circumstance affect your faith in God, because it is your real strength.

Those, who are strong and faithful, could face grief, pain, disgrace, and illness. The pursuit of joy and grief strengthens faith. It proves the true, strong worship of God.

Those, who have pure hearts and strong faith, are like an iron ball, which is stable in storms. Those, who are moved by their worldly desires, are like a dry leaf, blown easily by any gentle breeze.

Sai Baba finalises His words about faith, by saying that if the person loses his faith in God, he loses happiness and becomes a prey to anxiety. Life without faith is like water poured in a sieve. Happiness is only fulfilled through faith.

Surrender To God

"The Islam is to surrender to the One God. The person, who surrenders and devotes himself to God, lives in peace with society. He is the one, who is truly belonging to Islam."

Sai Baba

Many of the Sufis mentioned that the traveller in the spiritual path must cross seven basic degrees. These were mentioned by Imam Al-Ghazali in his book, 'The Sea Of Truth'. He spoke about seven seas, which must be crossed to reach the state of union with God. Farid Al-Din Al-Attar spoke about seven cities for the Divine Love. Al-Serag Al-Tousy mentioned in his book, 'Book Of Brilliance', these seven

Sufi Degrees, "Repentance - Piousness - Abstinence - Poverty - Patience - Surrender To God - Satisfaction."

The person, who surrenders himself to the Will of God, is the one, who has trust in God, and this is the sixth station for the Sufi Al-Ghazali. The seventh and last station is satisfaction. It is the crown of the trust in God. God the Almighty said,

> *"Those, who are faithful, submit to God!"*
> **(Al-Orman - 160)**

The one, who surrenders to God, takes Him as his responsible Master, where he asks His help, depends on Him, and leans on Him. God is his only Supporter and Defender. God, in His Holy Koran, taught us how to trust Him,

> *"He, who submits to God, He will be his supporter."*
> **(Al-Talaq - 3)**

The person, who reaches this degree, will always have submission to God, in misery and luxury, in distress and propriety, in health and illness, in fear and security, etc.

Islam And Surrender To God

Sai Baba describes Islam as the submission and complete surrender to the Will of God. The Islam is the complete surrender to God, the merciful, the powerful. He, Who provides us with safety and security. Surrender to God, as Sai Baba explains, is to surrender to Him in all our thoughts and acts, without waiting for any gift in return.

When surrender is complete, a direct bond exists between the person and God. Here, the person feels that God runs all matters. It is mentioned in the Holy Koran,

> *"He, who surrenders his face to God and is charitable, is folding tightly the middle bond and God is the only settler for all his affairs."* **(Lokman - 22)**

Sai Baba mentions that without surrender to God, we cannot free ourselves from slavery to our bodies. As long as we are attached to our narrow ego, it will surround us tightly with its walls and lock us in the prison of our bodies. We must penetrate this ego in front of God, the Almighty, saying, "It is You, the Almighty and this ego is nothing to us."

Sai Baba describes God as the Powerful and Knowing. We must worship God continuously, as long as we breathe and feel. We must think of nothing else, but God. We must do nothing else, except His orders. This is surrender and trust in God. After we reach the degree of trust in God, we will reach the degree of satisfaction. When the person faces in this world all sorts of misfortunes, their sourness vanishes by the warmth of satisfaction. He will then live in satisfaction and happiness. God, the Almighty, said in His Holy Koran,

> **"God is satisfied with them and they are satisfied in Him and this is the great victory."**
>
> **(Al-Maeida - 119)**

Mohammed, the Messenger of God, said, "If you are satisfied with what God gave, you will be the wealthiest of all people."

Sai Baba says, "No happiness is sweeter than satisfaction. The person seeks for happiness in different ways. No happiness is parallel to peace and no happiness is greater than the fruits of satisfaction."

The thought of evil, anxiety, fear, and disturbance leads to illness. Similarly, greed leads us to search for more wealth and fame. It takes us to distress and frustration. Satisfaction may only be reached through spiritual concepts. Do not encourage your wild desires. Be satisfied with what God offers you. You have enjoyed luxury and material things in your life, but you never reached peace. You must be satisfied with what you own now. If satisfaction leaks away from your heart, non-satisfaction will replace it. Desires lead to more desires. The human being, who has satisfaction and content, enjoys the happiness of the Godly Blessings.

Satisfaction is a high Degree. You must orient your minds towards satisfaction, in your journey ascending towards God. He, alone, could offer you peace.

Chapter - 8
Loving Allah

"Only thoughts of God and intense love for Him bring peace."

Sai Baba

The Divine Love is the highest sacred position for the Sufi Ibn Arabi. The proof of this love is God's sacred words,

"He loves them and they love Him." **(Al-Maeida - 54)**

The Messenger of God (Mohammed) called people for the love of God, saying, *"I ask You, My God, to make me love You more than myself, my vision, my family, my money, and the dripping of cool water to drink."*

In the pursuit of happiness, there are three main elements, something you do, something you are aspiring to do, and something you love. Love is the key to happiness. The spark of this love is ourselves, we ought to love ourselves first and above all, we should reach the state of self-satisfaction and conciliation with ourselves. Love does not necessarily take the shape of love between a human soul and another; it can be love of humanity or Divine Love, which is the wholehearted love of God and that simply is the concept of Sufism.

The concept of Divine Love in Islamic Sufism dated back to the revelation of the Holy Koran and we quote from the Muslims' holy book, one verse that defines the concept in question from Surah:

"If we love God, follow me. God will love you and forgive your sins. God is forgiving, merciful."
(The family of Imran - verse 31)

And from Islamic 'Sunna' and 'Hadith' (the teachings of Prophet Mohammed), in Hadith, Prophet Mohammed said about Faith, "Your love to God and His apostle Mohammed should transcend anything or anyone whomsoever."

Some went to say about Sufism that a 'Sufi' is one, who holds onto self-sacrifice and righteousness. We have on one hand the 'Sufistised', who reaches above Qualities by exerting his utmost and on the other, the Sufist, who is the one that mimics the 'Sufi' & the 'Sufistised' for the sake of renown. Some also said that the 'Sufi' is a one with unblemished soul and thus, comes to the fore in the hands of the whole truth (God). The one, who has untarnished faith in God, is 'safi' (pure-hearted). Others, who have true love for their beloved (God), are 'Sufis'.

Sufism, in fact, has many advantages. It's a kind of jagging for the human psyche that creates a dogged will-power deep down inside the human being; it also creates an individuality that aims to highlight the human aspect. Sufism disciplines the human character, until it reaches its ends by means of making use of its full potential. Sufism polishes and rectifies the human soul, the legacy of which is self-reassurance and certainty.

Sufism assuages men's stampede towards materialism. It also strikes a balance between men's materialistic preoccupations and his mundane burdens on one hand and on the other, between his spiritual needs, therefore offering man tranquillity and reassurance. This kind of reassurance represents itself in the form of intimacy between members of the Group.

The 'Sufistic experience' is a spiritual standing, in which the worshipper gets in touch with God. This is called 'the Condition' in 'Sufis' terms, out of which stems the Sufistic spiritual enlightenment. Love, in actual fact, is the most particular and supreme side in Sufism. It is an expression of the most violent dispositions inside a human soul. Love is the reason that made the Sufis synthesise the language of Divine love in the treasures of poems. The final aim of the Sufistic experience is the union between the Sufi (lover) and the beloved (God), when the devotion between the two peaks, the ego vanishes, thus transcending the world of mind and sensualities into the real world. Passion has a role to play here, where a strong desire surfaces, pushing the soul towards Divine love and devotion. The main objective of Divine love is to adrenalise emotional powers, shoeing them towards faith that intensifies little by little, so that the devotion to God grows to the degree of perfection, ending up as a continuous meditation in the Divine self that reaches absolute indulgence. The Sufi's main feeling is of a unique supreme being, God. He is as if he is one track minded and overwhelmed by the notion of a limitless love and devotion to God. Then, the day comes, in which the Sufi's heart and his love for God turns to be a love for the entire world with all its creatures.

A man loves his wife and vice versa. He loves his friends, siblings, and his folks. This love is a second degree love, as it is considered mundane, a love that flourished inside us just to make us feel happy and joyful. But, when this love is turned towards God, it becomes a first-degree love, where there is a permanent celebration of God and a ceaseless drift towards God. It is a special kind of love just for the mere sake of love itself. It's a sincere, pure-calibre love.

A Sufi fearlessly loves God, a love where there is no room for personal benefits or ego-centrism. The Sufi gives and doesn't expect anything in return. He yearns to be always in close communication with God through worship and continual prayers.

The Sufi never worries, he has no personal troubles or interest in life's misfortunes, as he is convinced that his beloved God is the One, Who bestows everything and being in constant devotion, nears God gradually by virtue of his profound love.

The Sufi tends to withdraw from the materialistic world during his spiritual journey. He considers this the keystone of spiritual enlightenment, where the soul attempts to go deeper inside the spiritual world at this point. The Sufi's spiritual growth swells, reaching the level of spiritual inspiration that makes the Sufi sense spiritual ecstasy. He is experiencing an ecstasy that out matches the ecstasy of the five human senses and the brain altogether and then, the Divine blessing surfaces and helps ease the constraints of spirit, therefore setting the spirit free of mundane conflicts. The Sufi has quite an outpouring of emotions towards God and as man plunges into sunshine and its warmth, if exposed to it, the devotee Sufi is overwhelmed and engulfed by the love of God and sheathed in Divine blessings, when he unlocks his soul to the influx of Divine mercy. The Sufi is not drawn to mundane conflicts. He can be a witness on the world as a bystander, who can view a myriad objects which cry for God and behind these material objects lies Divine love. The Sufi tries to evade clashes as much as he can, in order to transfix his senses towards the centre of gravity, which is God. Anything irrelevant to God is not a Sufi's concern. To him, except for God, everything is non-existent.

The Sufi reaches the peak of human love and feels the fraternity of the people. In every aspect and sign, he sees God. He always controls his emotions, channelling them towards God and on his way, he can feel the pain, when he is delayed in arriving at these high levels of love.

At this point, he feels the pleasure of pain and longing caused by the absence of the beloved, God, the essence of Sufistic love and devotion.

Once, a would-be Sufi approached his teacher, asking to learn the final and most supreme stages of Divine Love, as he knew well how to love God. The teacher's answer was a smile. The learner repeated the question. The teacher then guided his learner to a great river and held the learner's head under water, until he was about to drown. The learner rushed out of the water, gasping and filling his lungs with air. He asked his teacher the reason why he did that. "What was your most valuable need when you were under water?" asked the teacher. The learner replied, "A breath of air." "When your love of God is like your need for a breath of air when you were under water, then you'll gear yourself for the highest level of Divine Love and you'll be a true devotee."

On the Sufi's path for Divine Love, his tenacity to mundane objects melts down. He is more attached to God and His omnipresence. Then, both wills of the lover and the beloved are united to the degree of complete acquiescence to God's will. The Sufi, along his path, is more able to distinguish between the phony, ephemeral materialism and the everlasting true soul. Thus, he starts to desert all that is phony. Here, the phony ego slowly dies along his way in the spiritual path leading to God.

When this phony ego perishes, the true ego looms as the eternal soul and as one Sufi man put it, "I went so far away to nihilism, the ego vanished and then, the ego reappeared as everything that is living, when I saw nothing but God."

There is a breed of Sufis, who are called the 'working Sufis'. This breed hurls themselves upstream in life. They are carried by the current and overjoyed that they are part of this life. They fear not the hustle and bustle of life as they are transferred from one milieu to another, contented, well aware that the power that sets the universe in motion is supporting them. They work as hard as they can, exerting their utmost, sparing no effort to fend off any foreseen danger. For that reason, their output surpasses others and reward is not their concern anymore.

The working Sufi is fearless. He is intrepid as he realises that happiness does not involve certain circumstances. He trusts that he will come out of any kind of crisis safe and sound. He feels he is standing on solid ground as the powers of the universe are by his side, shoring him up. This feeling injects inside him unique courage and will power, which any ordinary person lacks. A man, who lives on the assumption that his happiness depends on his success in a certain job, lacks the unique courage and will power, which the Sufi enjoys.

The Sufi's asceticism triggers exceptional power inside of him, the power that the ordinary man lacks. The Sufi comes to the rescue of orphans, widows, and destitutes, as serving the needy, to him, is a kind of devotion to God.

The greatest thing in the world is not big minds; it's big hearts that are devoted to God.

The Sufis' devotion may come to God, when they are physically feeble and destitute, but inside their hearts, there is a profound love for God.

Those devotees may be poor, but they are rich in love. Ability to love is the most paramount value, even more valuable than the ability to judge. The devotee of God may have nothing but his wealth of wholehearted love for God.

True love is lucid. When the Sufi devotes himself to God, the more he offers God his wealth, body, mind, and devotion, the greater the freedom he gains, which makes him the master of a limitless empire. The more the ego vanishes inside him, the deeper the modesty and devotion will be. Loving God sets the Sufi free.

For the most humble of souls, loving God is so great an object that it adds benediction on the huddled masses, which surround this soul. The love that comes from the soul of one of God's messengers is enough to purge entire humanity on this planet. Without this love, humanity will start to disintegrate into chaos and darkness. It is Love and not the mind that elevates man to higher horizons. Love is the key behind the unity of the universe, which is bound by love. Resigning to God means knowing Him and knowing Him means loving Him. Through love of God, you reach a condition of spiritual perfection with the entire life. Then, a strong feeling of God soars inside you. It's a gift confined only to those true-hearted devotees. This is actually the key to open the magic door separating matter and soul. By opening this door, the soul transcends the boundaries of the 'phony ego'. Thus widening the realisation of God, the soul reaches spiritual enlightenment. The internal alchemy turns the entire existence into a Divine-oriented energy. In this process, love plays the key role.

In the American periodical, 'PSYCHOLOGY TODAY', a study appeared about the Sufi's meditation approach that requires active rhythmic movements, while concentrating upon the praise of God. This study has revealed that those, who exercise this practice, feel euphoric and experience physical and mental salubriousness.

In an Egyptian study conducted by the author of this book, in collaboration with Dr. Medhat Al-Shakankiri, Professor of Biochemistry, University of Almenia, seven males and females, who suffer hypertension, were examined by recording adrenaline concentration in their urine specimens. Those patients were subjected to a week-long, extensive religious programme, comprising: performing prayers at the right times, praising God after each prayer, reading the Holy Koran after dawn and evening prayers for half an hour, and fasting on Mondays and Thursdays. All the above rituals were to be performed along with constant thoughts of God.

When measuring adrenaline concentrations in the urine of the above patients in the wake of performing said rituals, within 24 hours, it has been found that adrenaline concentration has dropped at a rate of 94% its usual high rate. This result shows that constant praise of God in every prayer and reading the Holy Koran pushes down significantly the adrenaline levels. The bottom line is that high blood pressure gets back to normal levels through praise of God.

Direct your heart towards God. He's the One, Who opens your eyes to see the right path to take safely. Seek always your communion with God, for He is the Source, Essence, and Light of this life. The more you love God, the wider He encompasses you with His love and offers you His blessings, as well as opening the locks inside you to an influx of His mercy, knowledge, and potency that comprises everything. The more you open up to God, the stronger you feel spiritual purity. You'll be God's sense of hearing and vision.

The more the soul whole-heartedly loves God, the higher it rises to the degree of the 'perfect human being'. This is exactly the core and crux of Sufism, when the soul feels the unity of existence and the presence of God in everything. God grants the soul tranquillity. The soul sees the beauty of the Maker and the creatures with an open insight. It feels as well in perfect harmony with the universe, which consolidates his faith in God's mercy, intimacy, and gratification. Therefore, his heart is purged of the lusts of the flesh, landing in the world of the kingdom on high, where he breaks free from the limits of time and space, and his love and devotion reach the phase of Sufism. It is man's most supreme love of all.

God Is Love

Love for Sai Baba is the essence of every human being. Without it, no human being exists. This love is great and closely bound with God. It is the light. It is the feelings, consciousness, purity, and joy. God is love itself. He embraces everything with His broad compassion. He diffuses everything. He is everything and nothing is like Him. He is the strength and the moving force of everything and every living thing. This strength is only love. Sai Baba says, ***"Love is God. Live in this love."*** But, how can we live and practise that love in our lives? Sai gives the answer,

- *Life is a challenge, meet it.*
- *Life is a dream, realise it.*
- *Life is a game, play it.*
- *Life is love, enjoy it.*

Here, the daily practice of love proves the ensured wisdom in Sai sayings,

- *Start the day with love.*
- *Fill the day with love.*
- *Spend the day with love.*
- *End the day with love.*
- *For this is the way to God.*

For ***Sai Baba***, it is the strength of love that changes evil to good. The strength of love carries within itself a true force. The only force that you should ask from God is the force of love. Through it, you could attain all other forces.

Sai Baba remarks about the essence of the human being, saying, "The human being is the personification of love. The human is thirsty for love. He finds true happiness in giving and receiving, not demanding love. A person should love everybody, because they all came from the soul of God." Sai Baba advises those, who demand love, saying, "Love all humanity. Love springing from your hearts makes your words pretty."

The best spiritual discipline helping the human being in his life is love. Take care of the love seeds, which are adherent with your ego and transfer them to the love of the group surrounding you. Let it grow to love all humanity. Let its branches spread everywhere to embrace all things, all living things all around the world. Start with small love and end with plenty of love, with limited love to end with broad love. Sai Baba goes on saying,

- *See with the eyes of love.*
- *Hear with the ears of love.*
- *Work with the hand of love.*
- *Think of love.*
- *Feel love in every nerve.*

Sai Baba continues saying

- *Love knows no hatred.*
- *Love is free from all selfishness.*
- *Love is ever distant from anger.*
- *Love will never take.*
- *Love knows only giving.*
- *Love is God.*

Love And Peace

Sai Baba ensures that continuous peace cannot be obtained, except through the Love of God. Pure Love springs only from a peaceful heart.

Peace of the human being cannot be fulfilled, except through thinking of God and loving Him with great strength.

The Love of God makes you Divine and gives your life its meaning. Through this Love, you may obtain the blessings of God and enjoy calm peace.

Peace is a state of mind vacant from any thoughts. Within this peace, Divine Love develops. When this Love becomes a part of the thoughts and the mind, the human being is at peace.

Love is the only alchemy and the only solution in this age. It is the only weapon, with which you can fight evil.

Love is the most magnificent thing in the world. It can make great miracles in changing the nature and manners of the human being.

Love and Mercy are God. Knowing God cannot be fulfilled, except through Love.

Love is the width and expansion in life. Plant Love to flourish in the form of mercy and forgiveness, yielding the fruit of peace.

Chapter - 9
Serve All

"God's love is our motive to serve others, through which we obtain self peace."

Sai Baba

Service in the conditions of Ibn Arab in Sufism, is considered of the highest conditions, higher than the condition of meditation. God has urged the love of others in the Koran, in the story of Abu Talha, who invited a guest of the prophet for dinner and gave him all his children's food, preferring his guest over himself, as it is said in the Koran,

"Favour others over themselves, even if they are needy and he, who is spared stinginess, is the successful." (**Al-Hashr - 9**)

The prophet has advocated helping others and has set it at a higher level than worshipping in his saying, *"To walk with my brother for his help is better than keeping to my mosque for a month."*

Islam has taught us that visiting the ill is a dear duty for its positive effects on the patient, as it is also a means of mercy in helping others. For its importance, the prophet has recommended in his saying, transmitted by **Al-Bukhari** in the chapter 'Necessity of visiting the ill'.

"Feed the hungry, visit the ill, and liberate the war captive."

Also, what the prophet said of the divine saying, "My slave, I was sick and you did not visit Me." The slave says, "How can I visit You, God the Almighty?" God, the Almighty says, "My slave (named) got sick and you did not visit him. If you did, you would have found Me at his side."

Mohammed And Service

The greatest example in history on other's service and self-denial is the Prophet Mohammed, who would help the needy despite his own need. He would feed the hungry and sleep with hunger himself, never keeping any money for himself, visiting the sick and encouraging them. Some of the most precious aspects of his character are his great kindness to the poor, orphans, and widows. He would do his best, according to his honourable saying, *"The upper hand is better than the lower one. Start with your family. Best give away what you can spare. He, who shies away, is covered and satisfied by God and he, who does not ask, is fed by God."*

Mohammed was not made happy by food and clothes, nor was he made unhappy by hunger, rudeness, or dismissal and he was not happy by sons or made unhappy upon losing them. He was only happy through helping others. Therefore he said, "Every Muslim has to give away." They said, "What if he does not have?" He said, *"Let him work with his hand to avail himself and help others."* They said, "What if he did not find?" He said, *"Let him support the needy and those in trouble."* They said, "What if he could not?" He said, *"Let him be right and abstain from evil. These characters are a gift to others."*

It has been said that Abu Zarr said that, the Prophet said, *"Every self in every day has to give away."* He said, "I said to the prophet, 'How can we give away, if we have no money?'" He said, *"Giving away includes stating, 'Allahu Akbar (God the greatest), Subhan Allah (God the Almighty), Al-hamdulillah (Thanks God), La Ilaha Illallah (Nothing but God alone)', ask God forgiveness, order right, act against the wrong, clear people's path from dirt, bones, and stones, lead the blind, hear the deaf, guide them on their way and to whatever they may have lost that you know how to find, stand with them, who cry for your help, and support the weak with your arms. All of this is part of your giving away to yourself."*

Spiritualism And Service

Doctor Mohammed Sadek Aladawy mentioned in his writings about spiritual culture, that it is spiritualism, which directs man towards serving people and love, and that love is the meaning that man can develop and share with others in serving them. Service is a great attribute, it is the greatest value. Loving service only comes out of a kind self full of love and mercy for others.

Divine messages have urged man to train himself to love his neighbours as he loves himself and to offer service to those in need on a personal, social, and national level. By this way, peace is achieved in the world.

Man can make the meaning of religion clear and shining when love, mercy, and service are his main purpose in life. Service is the essence of every religion, as peoples' service is a service for their souls before their bodies. Today, people's bodies have become bodies in movable graves, obscured in their depths the truth of their existence. Their minds have darkened and their hearts are blind. They lived on Earth as the dead, with all God has given them of true life. This is grave agony for them, to be with themselves in graves for life. Trust, the secret which God wanted them to learn and to stand up for, was neglected. This is what we see in the majority, who stepped away from God, became stony-hearted and frigid, so that materialism swept them away from humanity.

The divine power guides service willing people to use what God bestowed upon them of talents and ability, to serve others. God's light is spreading and will keep on spreading through the increasing numbers of human heart candles, who love good and service. If man wants bigger strides on the path of light and peace, he has to increase his share of donating, helping with self-denial, and serving others.

Service is the real currency of spiritualism. It is within human service that man reveals the lofty meanings inside a generous human being. If man does not serve others and gives them his previously earned knowledge, then he is not truly alive and misses much of peace. When man has the honest will to serve others, God will manifest and appear through him, and He will also manifest in him the meaning of peace and the relationship with God.

The service currency is the essence of man dealings and the character of his life, which he spends happily whether in a book he writes, or in a kind word, even in a hand salute, or a hidden help to his brother man.

Self Love

The worst evil that could strike the human's self is selfishness, the biggest cause for all wrong doings. Selfishness makes man prefer his benefit to the privileges of the right and blinds him from what he should be, and lets him misjudge what is good, thus depriving him of inner peace. The greatest good in the human self is serving others by all charity, giving away and doing good. Others' service is the motto of every self that prefers others and seeks to serve them, to realise for them peace and tranquillity.

I... I... I... always this I. Psychologists think that most of the people, who always complain, are in reality the victims of self-pity, fear, in-tranquillity, and the most far from helping others. If we love God above self, love and get rid of selfishness, we reach the family level, and if we are liberated from bias of the family, we reach the level of patriotism. If we are liberated from our land, we reach the level of humanity and the universal unity of humanity and universal peace, regardless of man's country, origin, family, or his own self.

We have to get rid of all personal motives, whether caring about reward or punishment and hold for ourselves a special level that we believe in solidly and try to realise. Those, who work to benefit the larger part of human society, are considered to have possessed peace. They are mainly souls, who realise peace through knowledge. The degree of personality integration and its feeling of the social circuit are that the individual tries to make himself happy first, followed by those, who want happiness for his family, then happiness for his relatives, and then happiness for society in its largest context.

True spiritualism and true Sufism believe in the existence of divine power moving towards serving ethics in every man and urges to enable this power to act its joy in the best way. Helping others is a means towards spiritual progress. It is the most important element.

God And Service

Modern psychology proved that man's happiness and feeling of security and peace is only realised through his helping others. ***Sai Baba*** says that love is the motive for self-denial and the desire to serve others. Through this service, man gets inner peace. Man should not serve others for return, to attract attention or benefit, or to feel successful in work, or wealth, or power, but out of respect for others and for the sake of love.

When man endeavours modestly and purely to serve others and when he considers them his human brothers and sisters, God manifests in this service and comes close to this man to guide him and cover him with His love.

The aim of life is progress in love, enlargement of this love, and the vanishing of man in God's love. The best way to realise that is in serving others. Power is not helping only those, who help you, but those, who hurt you, although this is being considered dangerous nowadays. So, we have to use insight to assess how a man deserves service, before we serve him.

Keep busy with selfless service to others and you will be rewarded in time. Do service with all your heart and with complete satisfaction. This satisfaction will bring you peace and power.

What good is it to be a man, who does not come through living as an animal? Man is there to serve others. Every man has to serve his society in return for what he gets from it. This service has to be selfless to others, with the aim of sacrifice; then, it turns into a spiritual value.

Service exists for the society and society exists for the nation. Nations are parts of this world, which have to seek peace. Man has to realise that his soul exists in his body not for selfishness, but for serving others. Man gets his wealth, knowledge, and experience from society and has to pay back to the society, by doing good in return for receipt. Offer service to the helpless, needy, and miserable and when helping them, remember you are serving God. Those, who serve by thought, word, or action, are purifying their minds. By serving others, man develops his innate animal nature.

If selfishness, jealousy, and bad feeling fill ourselves, we cannot do good. If the pot is empty, fill it with good work. Take away bad feelings in yourselves and fill your heart with love and preference for others. Hearts immersed in love are sacred hearts.

Other service must be done with a preference for others. This service may be small, but if done with a big heart, brings wonderful results. We take care of our love at family level and this love must be enlarged to include society, the nation, and the world.

God manifests in others' service. The 'I' brings bad results, while preference for others brings good results. We have become servants and must remain servants, and have to aim at doing good through the feeling that we are God's servants, if we wish for the vanishing of our ego in God.

Today, the world is in rapid progress upwards and man's character is falling downwards. With sacrifice, man can develop his humanity and rise to Godly horizons. Insult of any man is insult to God. Hatred of any man is hatred of God. You have to serve your society by helping the poor and the needy. The human value of mercy is manifested by offering good to people, which means good to God. Service to others, if spread to reach every man, will be able to do away with hatred, envy, and greed that strike the world. Man, who always thinks of his body, family, wealth, and comfort is truly selfish. The only way to purify man's heart is through serving humanity. Prosperity of the nation and the whole world needs the spirit of service that comes out of strong enthusiasm, creative thinking, and noble motives.

Sai Baba finishes by saying that man, when serving others, has to do it to satisfy his feeling and not others, so that for man to realise himself, he has to consider that his service is for God's sake and that God is watching his actions.

Abdullah was sleeping in a corner of a mosque in Mecca, when he was awakened by the conversation of two angels above his head. They were preparing a list of the Blessed and one angel was telling the other that a certain Mahbub of Sikandar City deserved to be ranked first, even though he had not come on pilgrimage to the Holy City.

Hearing this, Abdullah went to Sikandar City and found out that he was a cobbler, repairing the shoes of people. He was famished and poor, for his earnings barely sufficed to keep flesh and bone together. He had, by severe sacrifice, piled up a few coppers during the course of years. One day, he spent the entire treasure to prepare a special dish, which he proposed to place before his wife as a surprise gift.

When he was heading home with the gift, he heard the cry of a starving beggar, who seemed to be suffering from extreme hunger. Mahbub could not proceed further; he gave the pot containing the costly delicacy to the man and sat by his side, enjoying the blossoming of satisfaction on his haggard face.

This act gave him a place of honour in the register of the Blessed. A place, which pilgrims to Mecca, who had spent millions of Dinars in charity, could not secure. The Lord cares for the feeling behind the act, not the fanfare and the fuss.

Chapter - 10
Non-Violence

"Non-violence is non-violence in thought, word, or action: in the sense that man is not the cause of harming another person by thought, word, or action."

Sai Baba

Violence is a hostile attitude, an off-spring of the feeling of hostility, and such a feeling of hostility can be directed towards nature, individuals, or communities. Violence is a response characterised by a strong reactive style, which might entail a reduction in the vision and thinking levels, and of communal violent attributes, which are an expression of the refusal of a status quo.

Violence is usually generated from feelings of anger, jealousy, spite, and envy. Given that the factors dominating violence are many, but in most cases, they are due to the degradation of the prevailing ethical values and the shaking of idols in the society. Development of the religious and the conscience traits in man is the best remedy against violence.

Islam has preached abandoning violence and its replacement with clemency, pardon, and forgiveness, following God the Almighty's saying,

"And those containing fury and pardoning people, and God likes the generous donors." (**Al-Imran - 134**)

Prophet Mohammed said, *"Should I let you know what glorifies the edifice and raises up the steps?"* They responded, "Yes, blessed Prophet," to which he said, *"That you be clement to who has ignorantly abused you, to forgive who has been unjust to you, to give to who deprived you, and to reproach who cessed you."* (narrated by Al-Tabarani) The blessed Prophet also said, *"The believer is not he, who stabs, nor he, who insults, debauchers, nor the flagrant."* (narrated by Al-Tormozi).

The Prophet Mohammed urged gentleness and abandonment of violence, saying, *"God is gentle and likes gentleness, and grants for gentleness what He does not grant for violence."*

Violence Genes

Scientists agree that violence is deep rooted in peoples' customs and traditions and consider that ethnic fanaticism of a race is none other than a communal subdivision process, and ethnic fanaticism is defined as allegiance to all that is within the community and hostility to all that is outside the community.

And this interprets the conflicts of groups within the community and the conflict of communities among themselves. Ethnic fanaticism is attributed to the isolation of communities and the development of some of their customs and traditions, to conserve their survival and to deep-root their identity in what renders them firmly holding onto the old customs and traditions. Except for a certain species of rats, there are no other vertebral animals that kill members of their same species and there is no other animal that finds joy in practising cruelty on another animal of the same species. The question here is why is violence and murder widespread in the human race? Man has practised many violent acts, wars and killed tremendous numbers of his same gender. Research scholars have tried to set up several interpretations for violent phenomena, which they attribute to communal, cultural, economical, political, and psychological reasons, in addition to another factor: namely, the dictatorship of rulers, their falling prey to grandeur and imposing dominance on peoples. There are, moreover, biological reasons for violence, which are instinctive; violence deep-rooted in the living organisms' hereditary genetic configuration, including the human race.

Non-Violence And Conscience

As regards violence, **Sai Baba** advises everyone to be timely in his speech and contemplate whether his words are painful to others.

Even man's look and thought must be free from violence. Man also must refrain from listening to evil speeches, because they harmfully affect him and detract him from his peace.

How do you consider and judge matters as good or as evil? This comes through consultation with your conscience. When you commit an act inconsistent with what your conscience dictates to you, this will be followed by undesirable results. Conscience is revelation of God within every human being. Anything you do, your conscience will tell you if it is right or wrong. Wait for some time and don't be hasty when talking, and when you hear something, test what you hear as to whether it is good or not. Then, decide what is suitable.

Non-violence in *Sai Baba*'s opinion is not merely in harming or hurting the feelings of others, non-violence is effective on man himself.

Non-violence is all that returns on man with happiness and peace. What harms man is considered violence. Man's life itself is governed by the principle of non-violence. And man has to be cautious in his food, because excess thereof is violence to the body and moderation therein results in benefit.

Sai Baba says that all types of violence in today's world are due to the fact that man does not live a righteous, pure life. People practise different kinds of worship and rituals, but they do not acquire peace.

God does not seek violence or bloodshed. Love is His instrument. Non-violence is His message. Egotism and materialism lead to violence and where social ethics worsen and character lacks, children appear not holding respect or concern for the elderly. Humanity and brotherhood have become unattainable dreams and it is good time that mankind awoke from its dormant state and rearranged its priorities, for at the terminal of the dark tunnel, we shall not encounter light should we not be disciplined and cooperative.

Society to date is divided and there is virtually no peace. The reason for that is ethnic differences and disagreements related to gender, language, and the surfacing of violence and conflicts. When violence is imposed to maintain world peace, such violence cannot stop adverse reactions.

Remedy Of Anger

Anger results in violence. Thenceforth, Sai Baba confirms that the angry man never acquires peace. Anger makes man commit many mistakes, frustrates his development and deprives him of others' respect. Anger causes destruction and the first fundamental principle for a man seeking spiritual development, is to control anger. When you feel angry, keep silent and remember God's name, and don't try remembering things that harm your mind and feelings. When anger is aroused in you, drink a glass of cold water, relax in calmness. Piously recite God's name. Walk a long distance speedily, so that thoughts distracting your patience convert into silence and isolation, whence the blood circulation activates and movement affects the tranquility of quiet thoughts.

At the moment when man loses his capacity for forgiveness, he is attacked by the thoughts of anger, hatred, and jealousy, which make him lose his humane nature and be engaged in evil thoughts, which drown him in a beastly nature.

Beware Of The Envious

Sai Baba says that man's life is unique. Life prolongs, when man is filled with happiness, calmness, and pure thoughts, but when man is filled with jealousy, anger, and hatred, his average lifespan shortens. The envious barely sleeps and insomnia destroys health more than does food. Envy is a fatal poison. It contaminates ethics, destroys character, and deprives you of peace. *Sai Baba* enquires, "What are man's robbers of peace and happiness? They are jealousy, anger, conceit, greed, and desire, which rob man's health and the worst of these robbers is envy." And it was thus said that you can make friends with an angry man, you can sleep beside a snake, but beware and don't make friends with an envious man.

Like you think, so you are. Our thoughts and acts are responsible for the virtue and the evil within us. Thinking with love leads to peace. Understanding with love leads to non-violence.

Peace And Forgiveness

Sai Baba says that forgiving people changes them as well as the forgiving person, who himself changes, so that if you are confronted with problems and difficulties, do not lose your temper and fall prey to depression. You should pardon and don't be tremulous, or allow the manifestation of anger, hatred, or retaliation, in moments of despair. Be firm and initiate with forgiveness and forgetfulness. The virtue of pardoning is man's greatest strength. If man waives this virtue, he turns into a devil.

Man should be attributed with humane virtues, but what we find today is jealousy dancing like devils all over the world. It is this jealousy and hatred, which makes people follow the path of evil and so, destroy themselves.

Peace and pardoning are two mutually consistent matters. Pardon is non-violence. It is sacrifice. It is the source of happiness and the third eye of every man.

Sai Baba concludes His word with an advice to the peace route treaders, by saying, "Don't try to look for others' wrong-doing, instead of yours, and you should implant three matters in your hearts:

- ***Do not forget God.***

- ***Do not toast the world you see around you, for this world is to perish, changing round the second and not continuous.***

- ***Do not be frightened, for inside you is the inappreciable soul.***

Sai Baba advises man to eliminate two things from his heart.

Forget any abuse directed towards you from any human being.

Forget the good deed that you have rendered to others.

It was quoted in the glorious Koran:

"And that you forgive is more approximate to piousness." **(Al-Bakara - 237)**

Chapter - 11
Health In Happiness And Peace

"There is no happiness greater than when man is satisfied. Man seeks happiness in its different forms, but there is no happiness equal to peace and there is no happiness greater than peace originating from satisfaction."

Sai Baba

"Inner peace is a basic factor in expediting man's recovery, particularly if complemented by deep faith in God's will, the magnificent Doctor, capable of curing illness and also, if added to that the full submission to God's might, curative to all illness."

Sai Baba

Happiness is linked in Islam with faith, for the faithful are blessed from God with happiness and He admits us to the eternal paradise, from the first instant after the end of the divine evaluation till eternity, except for the violating faithful, whom God wishes to delay in their admission to His paradise with their forerunners, for the time lasting their punishment, and God endows the lucky faithful in paradise a great and perpetual endowment non-diminished. It was quoted in the Glorious Koran,

"As for those, who have attained happiness, those are who are eternal in paradise as long as the heavens and the earth orbit, until your God wishes, blessed with an unlimited endowment." **(Hood - 108)**

It is God, Who has originated man from the void in the best build-up and has granted him guidance to what gives him happiness in this world, and that which follows, and it is God, Who has donated man food and drink, and enabled him to benefit from them in preservation to his right.

And if man falls ill, it is God, Who cures him by providing the means leading to remedy, deputing matters to His wisdom, and submitting to His might. It was mentioned in the Glorious Koran,

> *"He, who created me, He so guides me and He is, Who feeds me and provides me to drink, and if I am ill, He cures me."* **(Al-Sho'araa - 78-80)**

Alchemy Of Happiness

The alchemy of happiness is a spiritual remedy, which is one of the significant divisions of alternative medicine. This remedy generates the current of life's energy between soul and body, whence man fully reclaims equilibrium, harmony, and happiness through concentrating on God in piously reciting His name (Dhikr), contemplation, prayers, or reciting hymns in His glorification.

The alchemy of happiness was the old dream of the Arabs to convert cheap metal into a valuable metal, namely gold. And by applying the alchemy of happiness on man, one can convert the cheap, beastly aspect in man into a valuable, divinely spiritual aspect.

Islam's authority, **Hamed El Ghazaly** says on the alchemy of happiness that happiness is the art of recognising divine attributes, which are only realised within the heart. The alchemy of happiness liberates the heart from its beastly attributes by commemorating God.

The Muslim Sufi, Enayat Khan says that real happiness lies in the inner structure of man (the soul) and that all religious and spiritual philosophies have advocated that the path to happiness is the religious or Sufist path, and scholars have termed this path 'Alchemy'. He says also that, the Arabs have released symbolic narratives of Sufist concepts about the philosopher's stone, which converts cheap metal into valuable gold and that the search for gold as a metal would be the affair of those, who possess a curious sense, whereas for those, who have a sense of right within them, gold represents to them the spiritual light and inspiration.

Love and service are the philosopher's stone, says India's man of wisdom *Sai Baba,* and by which man's misery is converted into real happiness. The more man's heart is purified, the more increases its perception of divine superfluousness and his feeling of happiness magnifies. Through developing divine love, man's heart opens up and he feels a Godly happiness. Divine love is a lighthouse, which, if man directs his boat life towards it, will help him reach the harbour of happiness. The search for God in man's heart is that, which leads him to the real origin of happiness and man should spend every second of his time with the divine current, which emanates from God's name. Man must train himself to commemorate God's name with love, for this grants him perpetual happiness.

Service to others, says *Sai Baba*, is that, which helps in opening up man's feeling of God and introduces happiness in his heart. Offering service to others is the greatest means of man's advancement of the soul and is more than contemplating God and commemorating Him, and which man solely practises for his benefit and happiness and not for the happiness of others. *Sai Baba* repeats His guidance to people, saying, "Love all. Serve all," and His saying, "Help ever. Hurt never," and His saying, "Hands that help are holier than lips that pray."

Alchemy Of Man

> *Man is created from dust, air, and water. He grows by virtue of his food and God's alchemy leads to making up these elements void of life into a being pulsating with life. Man is his self's alchemist and all chemical changes inside his body continue unnoticed. Through this alchemy within him, which works behind a veil, this unseen alchemy is the*

eternal soul, which does not change and whose firebrand is associated with the greatest alchemist, who is 'God', the most proximate to his vein.

The aim of man's life is to know God. It is the last step of alchemy of happiness, which starts with knowing the self. The core of every human being is a part of the universe itself and when man perceives that, he will feel God as an eternal power, moving at an infinite speed within infinite dimensions.

Man And The Universe

The relation between intelligence and energy is manifested in the influence of the mind on matter. The universe as a whole has a spiritual divine nature and is governed by a constant divine law, and divine intelligence is present in all places and at all times. Such intelligence enables man to access it through meditation and contemplation.

Man is continually influenced by various forces surpassing the mind's perception and influenced with electromagnetic vibrations within and outside his body. Some of these powers have gainful effects, while others have destructive effects on man's health. There is an endless sea of molecules, which fill up man with their overflow, each one of them with its inner intelligence and a higher outer intelligence influencing it. The relation between man and the universe is firm indeed and such a man communicates with this universe through his higher self.

Man in this universe, despite his smallness and minority, is an important being, living for a temporary period at some place on planet Earth, which orbits in this endless space towards an unknown direction.

Man lives within a tremendous ocean of light of short frequencies and within this ocean are electromagnetic forces and radar waves, infrared and ultraviolet rays, x-rays and gamma rays extending to outer space, every wave having a frequency higher than that preceding it, and man's capabilities are too limited to discover all the different forces surrounding him.

Biofeedback

Man, an electrochemical being, has a soul, which is the true higher self, which employs the brain and the body with a clever mechanism to express itself during the lifespan of the body on Earth. Scientists have been able, nowadays, to discover the human brain's waves and have been successful in controlling both the mind and the body, and through observing mind waves, it is possible to train the control of them by man's will. Consequently, it is possible to consciously control the unconscious body systems, such as blood pressure, body temperature, muscle tension, and even gland secretions, and accordingly, heart diseases, blood circulation, and psychosomatic illnesses can be cured without any medicines or drugs, by control of the mind waves and training on biofeedback. This has opened up new doorways to the mind in view of enhancing its capabilities of memory, vision, education, and intellect.

Innovation: This scientific discovery confirms that the mind is capable of dominating the body, as well as confirming the capability of man through peace of mind to cure himself from various diseases.

Mind Waves

A new science, termed Alphagenics, has been developed, which specialises in the study of the brain's electrochemical activity and controlling its waves. The brain needing a continual and tremendous amount of energy to conserve its function, such energy can be measured with a brain scanner, which registers the waves emitted from the brain in accordance to its increase or decrease.

And in case of man's full consciousness, beta-waves are emitted from the brain on the brain scanner, in the form of fast positive and negative lines (Fig. 1). The variations in energy levels are only slight.

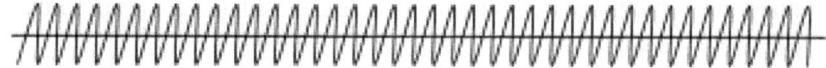

Figure (1): Beta Brain-wave levels maintain a fairly constant of energy through the brain.

When man's consciousness state changes through hypnosis, autosuggestion, pious prayers, commemoration of God, or contemplation of God, the brain wave levels transform into a state of alpha and theta waves (Fig. 2).

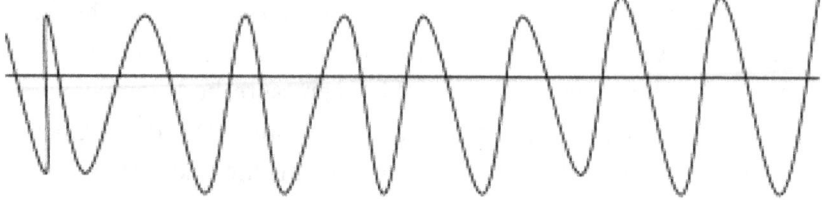

Figure (2) : Alpha and theta brain wave levels create large fluctuations of energy

The brain undergoes an 'altered state of conscience', which in turn leads to a major change in the energy levels, in which man feels inner peace, relaxation, and restitution. Alpha-waves deal with the internal levels of man's mind activity, in which man experiences calmness, inspiration, and creative innovative capabilities, as well as the process of curing illness, telepathy, memory, learning capabilities, day dreaming, awareness, and imagination. The alpha wave-length is beneficial to experience and to deeply conform with, whereas theta waves are manifested in states of deep meditation and contemplation, and in which man can dominate pain, recognise himself, and experience the cosmic feeling of God. There are also delta waves, which appear in cases of deep sleep and function in cases of unconsciousness.

When man's feelings are disturbed and a situation of tension and anxiety arouse him, his brain transfers spontaneously to the beta waves and in the case of strong faith in God and full submission to His will, man is accompanied with an inner peace emanating from divine love and the service of others, good-doing, pious prayer, commemorating God, and deep thinking and contemplation of God. In such cases, man's brain transfers to and conforms with the beneficial alpha-wave levels.

The adjusting of mind waves and consequently, brain chemistry plays a major role in finding mental peace and consequently, positively influences man's psychological and corporal well-being. Today's world is filled with drug addiction, violence, and terrorism, and the sole effective remedy is a spiritual Sufist awakening, through which man reclaims his psychological and spiritual equilibrium.

Groups Of Rituals

Man prays and prays and makes many 'Omra' visits and pilgrimages, but alas, finds that God does not fulfill his prayers. The reason for that is the person's prayers are artificial and void of spiritual faithfulness, and he lacks goodness and the warmth of divine love, which has cut off his firm relation with God within him and which is closer to him than his vein cord. We note here what was written about Abal Yazeed Al Bastamy, who wished to travel to El Ka'aba to perform his pilgrimage rituals. When he reached El Basra, he visited a famous Sufi of the Basra people. When the Darwish Sufi asked him, "What do you want, Abal Yazeed?" El Bastamy said, "I want to visit Mecca, God's shrine." The Darwish said, "Do you have your food and drink for this journey?" El Bastamy said, "Yes." El Darwish asked, "For what value?" El Bastamy said, "200 Dirhams." El Darwish said, "Abal Yazeed, my heart is God's house and El Ka'aba is God's house, with one difference being that God did not enter El Ka'aba after He built it, but He did not go out of my heart when He built it."

What did this Darwish want from Abal Yazeed Al Bastamy? Was what he said a trick of poor people's tricks? This is unlikely as the Darwish has returned Abal Yazeed's money. Most probably, the Darwish has advised Al Bastamy not to be a slave of rituals and to know that taking care of the poor is no less important than going around Al Ka'aba. This story was told by Shams El Din Al Tabrisi to confirm the importance of the human heart in the world of reality.

God says, in the divine saying, *"I have not been contained by My Earth or My skies, but by the heart of My faithful slave."* Ninety percent of sick people miss self-peace. They are somatically sick as they are sick in their thoughts and emotions and missing mental and spiritual balance. Most of those sick have their minds full of thoughts of selfishness, fear, dissatisfaction, and envy. The big sickness of this age is a spiritual sickness. The only cure is to bring inner peace into man's mind through large doses of love, honesty, good work, non-aggression, and service to others.

Man's Health

Sai Baba says that in his search to increase his wealth, man's mind misses quiet sleep, he reaches for drugs, which are poisons, which ruin an appreciable portion of man's health and make him subject to high blood pressure and heart disease.

Man's life is like a boat crossing a river, one bank represents the material world, the other the spiritual heaven that he wants to reach. The boat represents man's body. If they both develop a hole in the middle of the journey, catastrophe will occur and he wouldn't be able to complete his journey and reach the other bank.

The secret behind the complete health of the man is in preserving always a joyful mind that does not strain or hurry, a mind free from pressures of fear and worry, but today's man is always in a hurry, which causes him worry that affects his health. Changing man's mind will help him to realise health. But, how can this be achieved? This can be done by controlling emotions and feelings. Mental stress destroys man's health. Therefore, man has to learn the art of controlling feelings and emotions, for uncontrolled emotions stress the mind.

Limiting anxiety keeps illness away, but humanity today gets more worried about a lot of things, such as information from radio, TV, papers. The news media causes fear and dissatisfaction, thus increasing anxiety. Here, the mind is affected by fear, which is the cause of sickness. The cause of illness may also be a direct result of permissions. Man's health comes from a stable way of life. If you serve yourself rather than servants, your health will improve. A lot of heart problems are due to hurry, worry, and rich food. Hurry strains body organs, so it affects the heart. Worry causes a lot of illness, including ulcers. Excessive rich food raises the cholesterol level and causes heart diseases. By avoiding excessive strain and controlling food habits, man can keep up good health. Sai Baba wonders about the man, who wants peace while he cultivates worry, like the man, who grows a lemon tree and hopes to get mango fruit, which indicates absurd ignorance and blind insight.

Health And Food

Sai Baba says that most seekers to God look upon food as unimportant. As body and mind are closely connected, food should not be ignored. Food affects the mind, thoughts, and actions. Food is an important factor in controlling alertness, sluggishness, worry or calm, happiness or sadness. Food categories are divided into three types:

First Type: Promoting Emotions

Very hot foods and rich in spices and fat. This type excites man's feelings, generates anger, arrogance, and selfishness. This includes fish, eggs, meat, pickles, spices, tea, coffee, coca, and sugar.

Second Type: Promoting Dullness

Very salty food and very spicy food well cooked. This type induces sleep, laziness, and sluggishness. It includes can foods, meat, pork, wines, onions, garlic, tobacco, and narcotics.

Third Type: Promoting Love, Peace, And Happiness

Balanced food that is not very hot and not very spicy. It is light on the stomach, causes no indigestion, and is easy to dispose of. It does not hurt the mind, but helps peace and quietness, necessary for meditation and spiritual exercises. It includes milk, cheese, butter, fruits, vegetables, dried fruits, nuts, rice, raw sugar, ginger, and honey.

Most diseases come from excessive eating. Most people eat three meals and maybe four or five per day. The yogi eats only once at noon time. At least, it is preferred to have two meals at 9:30 a.m. and 6:30 p.m. in this system.

Relation Between The Brain And Love

The human self is very complex, swinging between love and hate. When man misses love and human feelings, man develops psychological and bodily sicknesses. Therefore, love is considered a curing elixir from age old diseases.

There is a close relationship between the brain and love. The brain is a divine miracle full of secrets that cannot keep action of its cells, unless it gets its share of sympathy and love. Without love, it turns into a machine with weakened capabilities that can't resist disease. Because the brain controls body organs, if it gets well, all organs get well too. If it suffers from lack of emotions and love, it is disturbed and all organs are disturbed as well, and it will manifest psychosomatic problems. The brain that gets what it needs of true love gives longer and healthier life to its owner.

Love is one of the most important human relations, which gives us the ability to keep on living and helps us endure life's hardness. It is the basic source of our mental and psychological balance, very important to health and long life. Spiritual life should not keep man from actively participating in life in society. *Sai Baba* says that man can keep his head in solitude and his hands in society. So, we must not turn our backs to society, searching for spiritualism. Work we can do spiritually and the same with our duties to family and society. *Sai Baba* advises us to keep on praying, contemplating on God and meditating on God, seeking God's countenance with complete surrender to the Almighty God.

Contemplating God and meditating on God purifies the depths of the mind, so it is saturated with purity and power, and consequently, is filled by satisfaction and peace, which brings good health to man.

Body and mind depend upon each other. Complete dependence on divine love expedites man's recovery. This love stems out of the divine torch that is within us.

The Healing Power Of Doing Good

Harmony, compatibility, and love will bring reconciliation with the self. Man is naturally inclined towards goodness. He reverts to evil only under pressure or temptations against this nature.

Doing good, in every way, brings satisfaction, comfort, and tranquillity to a man, which leads to psychological stability and diminishes any psychological disturbances. Psychological health is the result of many factors. Doing good is at the top of these factors, as it is compatible with the divine system, its soul and its kind human aims.

In recent research on immunology, it has been proven that doing good is more beneficial to its doer himself. Doing good and charities are some of the curing elements prescribed by doctors for sick people.

Scientists confirm that love of good and good deeds bring great benefit to the immune system, which is related closely to self stability, since nerves connect the brain and the bone marrow. Recent treatment for sick people is to encourage them to help others to improve their psychological states and hence, their physical condition, thus strengthening their immune system. Helping others without direct interest expedites recovery and helps heal psychological and bodily wounds. Preference for others has its positive effects.

It has been found that urging patients, who suffer from psychological pressure, to give results in helping them overcome their problems. This could come as a result of producing endorphins in the brain, which are normally produced when feeling psychologically comfortable. Scientific studies have proved that helping others increases the level of man's health. Abundant health is not realised, unless man feels connected to something outside himself. Man's systematic helping of others has a great effect on his health, comparable to his keeping up with regular sports and good food. Self denial, love, and kindness is the curing balsam that breaks the deadly circle of fear and strain. Love and service of others is the strong curing medicine, opposing and acting against reluctance in sharing with others. Change of mind from 'I' and 'they' to 'We' strengthens man's feeling of society. Helping others, such as taking care of children, reading for the blind, and visiting old people, brings good health to man. Man needs to meet with whom he helps, see their life, and feel for them. Love feelings in our personal contact with others increases our understanding and sympathy for them, which decreases our feelings of loneliness and strengthens our link to the greater human society.

Medical studies have proved that doing good and helping others brings good health to those, who do it just like physical exercises. There are proofs that helping others lead to the following changes:

Physiological Changes	**Psychiatric Changes**
- Strength in the immune system.	- Feeling refreshed.
	- Feeling high spirited.
- Less pain.	- Being more active.
- Control of weight.	- Feeling of tranquillity.
- Less insomnia.	- Feeling more relaxed.
- Less spread of tumours.	- More happiness.
- Improvement in the heart.	- Optimism.
- Less acidity in the stomach.	- Great feeling of well being.
- Lower blood pressure.	- Less lonely.
- Less consumption of oxygen.	- Decrease in aggression.
- Faster healing after surgery.	- Decrease in feeling helpless.
- Better blood circulation.	- Feeling healthy.

- Betterment of Rheumatism.
- Improvement in breathing.
- Most of them with long life.

- Feeling connected to others.
- Belonging to a larger spiritual family.
- Feeling of inner peace.

The Curing Treatment

In relation of the mind to sickness, **Sai Baba** says that relation is close between weak mind and sickness. The mind is weak, when struck by worry, hatred, and bias. These feelings finally cause contamination of the mind. Modern civilisation has a difficult role, in that eye is contaminated by watching films of violence and sex on TV. The ear is polluted by listening to loud music and news of accidents and catastrophes. Man has to avoid listening to bad news, like a collapsing economy, killing, and violence, as it causes him fear and insecurity and thus, sickness. Man has to rid his mind of thoughts of fear and worry and replace them with positive thoughts full of values and spiritual principles. The hours that man spends with God supply him with power, strength, and enable him to sustain life's hardships and pain. Thinking of God is the curing treatment of all diseases. Instead of buying medicines, drugs, and expensive vitamins, there is one vitamin that cures sickness. It exists in 'God'. Its most important element is divine love, honesty, good work, peace, and non-violence. If man is interested in good characteristics and manifests them in his character, and helps his brother man, he won't have any vitamin shortage and will achieve a high level of mental and physical health. Spiritualism is only a simple style in life. This style is materialised, when man keeps a kind heart and sympathises with others. This basis of sound spiritual life is existent in purity of thought, good taste in speech, and good work.

The surrender of human will to the divine power will raise the standard of thoughts, words, and actions to the level of worship.

Man's thoughts, words, and actions must be founded on divine love and love of all creatures created by God. Love is the essence of every living being. This love is simple, natural, and shines with goodness, mercy, and sympathy. If man cannot feel pure love for all, the least he can do is not hate or intend evil to another man. Speak softly, do not talk much, and in the depths of silence, you can hear the voice of God.

Chapter - 12
The Self-Peace Path

This work is a collection of Sri Sathya Sai Baba's writings that are being brought out, in an effort to assemble together important **Peace** facets of His message, from:

Dharma Vahini

Dhyana Vahini

Leela Kaivalya Vahini

Jnana Vahini

Prasanthi Vahini

Prema Vahini

Sathya Sai Vahini

Vidya Vahini

Sutra Vahini

Upanishad Vahini

Swami's direction and advice help the **Peace** seeker to proceed, until Inner Peace is attained. Let us read it with care and practise it. He will bless our Journey to **Self-Peace**.

The person, who is free from all desire, who has not even the slightest inclination to possess or enjoy the sensory world, who has no trace of egoism or possessiveness, who is ever in the bliss of God-consciousness, far from any tinge of sorrow, he is established in supreme joy and peace. At least in his last moments, if a man is fixed in the knowledge of his basic nature, which is Divine, he can successfully merge with that, beyond a doubt.

What is the goal of human life? What is the objective that man must realise? Is it just eating, drinking, sleeping, tasting a little joy and grief, and finally dying, like any bird or beast? No, certainly not. A little thought will reveal that it is not so. The goal is the realisation of the Absolute, of God! Without that, no man can attain peace. He must win that Bliss of Divine Grace. However much one strives to extract happiness from the multiplicity of worldly things, the quantum of satisfaction is very little; as for Peace, one finds it is impossible to get it through the things of the world. The mind can have peace only when it merges with the Absolute Consciousness, the Primal Cause, the Unchanging Existence.

Even the most comfortable house, equipped with all the luxuries man craves for, even heaps of treasure, are helpless to endow one with peace. That can be won only by surrender to God, Who is the very core of one's being, the very source of all life. Consider this: Do those, who are lucky enough to possess wealth, gold, property, and comfort, have peace? Nor is this all. Are men, who are highly learned or persons of extraordinary beauty, or super-human physical strength, at peace within themselves and the world? What is the reason for the misery of even these?

The reason is: they have forgotten the Divine basis of Creation. They have ignored the one Absolute Underlying Principle. All lives, lived without Faith and Divine Love to the One Supreme Overlord, are despicable; lives spent without tasting the Nectar of the Divine Principle are all wasted chances.

If everyone treads this holy path, the Lord Himself will bestow on each all that is needed, all that is deserved, and all that will give peace of mind. Offer everything to the Lord without any desire for the result; that indeed yields full joy; that is indeed the easiest.

In the confusion of overpowering events, we see men sometimes placing faith in others, who are noisy and enslaved by their own passions. But, this is a passing phase. It will not last. When things are tranquil, calm, and unruffled, man can merge in the atmosphere of illusionless, pure consciousness; this is the highest he can reach. The peace he tastes here is subtler than the subtlest. He must ascend to it through effort guided by reason, through meditation on God. When the enjoyment is full and complete, it is no other than the Divine status, the coveted Goal of Life. Men do not generally strive for it, because they know nothing of its supreme attraction. Meditation on God gives them the first inkling of that Bliss.

Another special thing about invocation is this: it is possible to acquire various occult powers through Yoga and Tapas. So, there is every likelihood of the Lord being forgotten when these powers come. Blinded by this pride, a person might even let go the basic victory won by his spiritual practice. This is not the case with God's Name, Invocation, and Meditation on God; no such dangers beset those paths. These three make Divine Love grow in man more and more. Through Divine Love, peace is achieved. Once Peace of Mind is achieved, all other conditions are attained automatically. Through Yoga and Penance, extraordinary Power; through recollection, invocation, and meditation on God, extraordinary Divine Love - this is the difference between the two.

Never think about the badness or evil of others. If you can manage it, keep always trying to turn them into good ways and giving them good advice. One should cultivate peace of mind, charitableness, and the eagerness to promote the welfare of all. These can come only through invocation and meditation on God. The wealth derived from invocation and meditation on God is Good Qualities. They clean the exterior, they purify and enable the inner tendencies also.

One should have the desire only for the path of Realisation. One should not dedicate one's life for the mean desires of the world. Dedicate all to the Lord; this is genuine contentment, the result of acquiring peace of mind, joy, and discrimination. Of peace, contentment, and inquiry, God realisation is also possible then.

To acquire peace and contentment, recollection and meditation on God are the only means. They alone can give power. Nowhere else can you find them. More than anything, if you possess contentment, the other two will be added to you. Nothing is more profitable to man than contentment. It is a treasure richer than the three worlds. The contented person can experience indescribable Divine glory. He is more joyful than the owner of the wish fulfilling cow and wish fulfilling tree. He can immerse within himself and discover bliss. Do not strive for physical joy, discarding the more permanent joy of inner calm and contentment.

Every man must develop the virtue of contentment, through meditation of God-Practice. Contentment is a Pure quality; it will not transform you into an idler; no, not at all! It will, on the other hand, permit the mind to travel towards the Lord; it will grant peace. It will also hinder inessential activities, which have profit for oneself as the aim. The contented man will be fully pure; he will lead an inner life, in communion with the soul. He can do any work, without rest and without complaint. The waves of the mind, which sway in many directions, have a single aim. The Sages and Yogis of the past realised the goal of life by means of the peace that came to them through Contentment.

The seeker has to be ever watchful of the fickle tendency of his mind. When the mind flits from object to object, he must bring it back to the right path and to the right object. That is the correct spiritual practice, the path of concentration and meditation. If, however, the seeker does not struggle to achieve this one-pointedness, but leaves the mind to itself, following vagaries from this to that, this is called monkey-meditation; a type of meditation, which is very harmful indeed to spiritual progress.

In short, the chief purpose of Concentration and Meditation on God is to minimise the travels of the mind and force it to stay in one place. Holding it on that fixed stage, one should continue spiritual practice for a long time. Then, there is no limit to the peace and joy that one can have.

Without meditation on God, no one can achieve the experience of the Godhead. Advise the mind, which flows so swiftly in so many directions, "Oh Mind, do not drag me along the flood of objects, along the path of sensual desires and spoil my career. Take me to the Lord instead. Flow in that direction, please." Giving up all other desires and ever content, dwell on His Name and His Form only, to the exclusion of everything else. Meditation on these is real peace, genuine Contentment.

Do not worry about the unsatisfactory environment you may have. Of course, the place may have some drawbacks and it may not be ideal. But, it is no use trying to run away from all that. You can overcome the drawbacks by training your own mind. Stay there itself and pray to the Lord! Pray that He may fill you with His thoughts and vision, making you ignore the defects of the environment. Do not seek comfort, for comfort might not be conducive to meditation. Learn to be comfortable in any place; that is better. Live in joy wherever you are; that is the way. Revel in the realm of your mind; worship there the Lord you have chosen as your goal and be free of all the defects of the natural or human environment! No sport can then be irksome to you, nor will any place seem disgusting.

He, who has subdued his mind, will be the same in good times and in bad. Grief and joy are but aberrations of the mind. It is only when the mind is associated with the senses and the body that it is affected, agitated, and modified. When one takes in an intoxicant, one is not aware of pain, is it not? How does this happen? The mind is then detached from the body and so, it is not bothered by physical pain or discomfort. Similarly, the Jnani too has immersed his mind in the Self; he can establish mental peace and quiet by disciplining the mind.

A word to those, who are overwhelmed by the burden of worldly responsibilities and anxieties and to those, who find themselves unable to pray to the Highest, either because they have condemned themselves undeserving, or because they have no faith in the Highest: Enormous is the number of those, who live their days in joy. You, too, were joyful and are so, now. But, everyone is destined to disappear one day, as generations have already done. Therefore, everyone must desire and adopt every means to attain not only joy, but what is far more valuable - peace of mind and an ideal, exemplary life.

Peace must be manifested in feeling, word, posture, and deed; in the same uniform equal measure. Then, Peace becomes inner peace, the Real peace. Bereft of such Peace, one cannot hope to get either worldly or trans-worldly bliss. Peace is the nursery of all happiness and all joy.

There are no drugs, which will cure this dreaded disease. No other means can ameliorate the illness. To get peace, love is the only means. Divine love yields the divine flame of peace. Peace brings about unity of all mankind and this unity combined with spiritual knowledge will bring about world peace.

The discipline of the self is the basic foundation for successful living. Through that alone can man attain real and lasting Peace. And, without peace, there can be no happiness. Peace is the very nature of the Self. It co-exists only with a pure heart; it is never associated with a greedy heart full of desires. Peace is the distinguishing mark of Yogis and sages. It does not depend on external conditions. It will flee away from the selfish and the sensual. It hates the company of such persons. It is the characteristic of the Inner Soul, wonderful, unshakable, and permanent.

Peace is full of spiritual uplift and wisdom, the natural accompaniment of bliss. Genuine Peace is won by the control of the senses only. Then, it can be called Inner Peace. The experience of that stage is as the Stream of Peace. Calming the mental agitation that surges like waves, levelling the swirls and whirls of likes, dislikes, love, hate, sorrow, joy, hope, despair, only then is peace earned and maintained without disturbance. Peace is of the nature of the Self. The Self is imperishable. It does not die like the body and mind. It is universal, it is subtle, and its very nature is knowledge. So, peace also partakes of these characteristics. Knowledge of the Self destroys illusion, doubt, and sorrow. Hence, Self-Knowledge confers the steadiest peace and with it, Holiness and Happiness.

If you yourself have no peace, how can you ensure world peace? Those enthusiastic about world peace must first learn how to experience and enjoy the peace themselves. Later, they can spread that peace to the world outside them and help to promote it.

Everywhere now, one can hear the cry, "World Peace," "World Peace," but the number of persons, who can tell how it can be attained is very small! There is no one, who can even picture correctly what exactly is meant by peace. For, if one has acquired true peace and experienced it, the turmoils and confusions of the world will not be cognised at all. You cannot be aware of its absence, if you have it. Peace means, "The giving up of the activities of the senses," which can be experienced, but is incapable of being exchanged from person to person. The best that can be done is to show the way to others, to inform others of its sweetness. How can another's hunger be appeased by your eating your food? The diner alone derives satisfaction from the dinner. Peace, too, is of such a nature. Each has to earn and experience it for himself, so that all may have it. Love and Fortitude are enough to confer peace. But, you should not concentrate on mere outward show; let these virtues saturate your thought, word, and deed; that is the way to establish world peace also.

Certain people declare that Prayer can bring about world peace and they ask people to pray. Of course, it is good to pray, but Peace can never be gained by that alone. Prayer must be united with practice. You should not pray for one thing and practise another. Such prayer is only a means of deception. The words you utter, the deeds you do, the Prayers you make must all be directed along the same path. While repeating prayers for World Peace, if you cannot patiently put up with others, if you slander others and look down upon them, you yourself will have no peace; you will have turmoil, instead! And with the turmoil, all the attending sorrow and pain!

Man is a bundle of impulses and intentions. He reduces his innate divinity and inner peace by giving free vent to these two. The impulses are the fuel, the intentions are the fire. The fire can be put out only by placing the fuel aside. The dying down of the fire is the attainment of peace. Dive deep into the ocean of peace and earn the invaluable pearl, the Bliss of the Spirit. When that opportunity is seized, man becomes the personification of the effulgent, holy state of peace. That is why the Vedas declare that Man is the embodiment of peace. Therefore, you should not delude yourself by imagining that you are the seat of disquiet and untruth. Know that you are the embodiment of peace, that Love is the blood that flows in your veins, and that your very nature is Joy; realise this by actual practice and experience.

Without peace, it is impossible to see the Truth. As the rays of the Sun are for the blossoming flower and the ripening fruit, so are the rays of peace necessary for the full development of Man. Then only can he ripen into the realisation of the true, the eternal, the blissful Brahman.

All the senses, all the impulses rise up in overpowering strength like waves from the sea, roar in fury, and subside in the waters; they do not confer peace. The wise thing is to forget these waves and to direct attention towards the sea beneath, which is without change. Then only can you attain Peace, swim about happily in the deep, undisturbed waters.

When man is immersed in Peace, he will experience the joy and exhilaration of that state in all ways. A person, who has tasted that joy and exhilaration, can never tolerate even for a second the state of Agitated mind and he will never desert the peace stage. If it ever happens that he is forced into Agitated mind, he will struggle furiously and desperately to return to the state of peace and might even die in the attempt.

The Self-Peace Path

You should always strive to change the course of the senses and the imagination to subjects and desires, that are conducive to the ideal, whatever be the difficulty, however serious the crisis. That is the sign of real intelligence; that is the road to real peace.

One must be surrounded by experienced men and men, who are basic supports of a good life. One must grasp the Reality with their help and experience the Reality oneself. Then only can Peace be established in the personality.

If the ignorance surrounding the Self is destroyed by wisdom, then everything will be illumined as at sunrise and Peace will be the result. If the above result has to be attained, some effort has to be made to provide the necessary conditions. The mind is conditioned into good or bad, by the environment. Hence, man has to create for himself the environment he needs. The reformers of today do not strive to transform the qualities of man. They try to bring about equality in economic matters, in outer life. But, these can be lasting only when the qualities of character are built on the basis of equality. If the quality of equality is not developed, even if everything is divided and shared equally, that state of equality cannot last. So, there is need to reform the character by means of the knowledge of the Self. This reform alone will bear fruit, the fruit of peace.

The Self is misleadingly denoted by the word 'I'. How can the seen be the seer, the eternal? How can the body be the real I? When this mistake is made, there can be no peace and no joy. It is only when this truth is understood and experienced that one can have peace.

May all Seekers, by their disciplined lives and ceaseless effort, establish themselves in the knowledge of their own True entity, their own Reality. May they keep their minds away from the seen world, contemplate on the Universal Soul always, acquire peace of mind, withdraw from all contact with the sensory world, saturate themselves in Bliss, and know themselves as the One without a second.

When I see the heaps of books that lie around everywhere, I feel that the wisdom inside the book cannot succeed in penetrating the heavy binding and emerge into the light. God is hidden by these huge heaps of books. Though these books have spread to all corners of the Earth, we cannot say that culture has increased or that wisdom has increased; man is still not far from the ape. An attractive binding and title, a beautiful picture, these are what the reader seeks, viz. transitory pleasure and momentary contentment. Only those, who, by means of discrimination, select the books they read and practise what they read, can realise the Truth and enjoy everlasting Bliss. Only they live worthy lives. So, those, who seek the highest path and who revel in thoughts of God, should strive to read only the life histories of saints and sages and the books, which help the contemplation of the Divine. Aimless reading of all and sundry books and whatever comes to hand will make confusion only worse. It gives no profit, confers no peace.

The nature and condition of the spiritual path are known only to those, who have journeyed along the road. They know that the path of Truth and Discrimination leads to Universal Soul. Those, who have not trodden that and those, who are not aware of its existence cannot explain it to themselves or to others.

The Universal Soul alone is real. The Universal Soul is Truth. The Universal Soul is Love. Meditate on Him as Truth, as Love. It is possible to realise Him in whatever form you meditate upon. Be always in the company of His devotees. Through this, discrimination and detachment will be implanted and increased. These will strengthen the spirit and endow you with inner peace. Your mind will then merge in the Universal Soul.

Every aspirant, who seeks the eternal through the path of Divine Love, should strive to acquire the following characteristics: He must keep away from the turmoils, the cruelties, and the falsehoods of this world and practise truth, righteousness, love, and peace. This is indeed the path of Divine Love. Those, who seek union with God, those, who seek the welfare of the world, should discard as worthless both praise and blame, appreciation and derision, prosperity and adversity. They should courageously keep steady faith in their own innate reality and dedicate themselves to spiritual uplift.

Joy and peace do not inhere in external objects; they are in yourself. But, people in their foolishness search for those outside themselves, in a world, from which, today or tomorrow, they are bound to depart. Therefore, awake soon. Try to know the essence of everything; the eternal truth. Try to experience Love, which is the Universal Soul itself. Discriminate at every turn, accepting what is true and discarding the rest. So long as one has worldly desires in view, he cannot escape sorrow.

Permanent happiness can be secured only through one Vidya, the Upanishad Vidya. That is the science of God-realisation that is the Teaching of the sages. That alone can save Man and grant him peace. There is nothing higher than that; this is an indisputable fact. Whatever your joy and sorrow, whatever the subjects you have specialised in for a living, have your eyes riveted on God realisation. If intelligence alone is sharpened, without the growth and practice of virtues, and if mere information is stored in the brain, the world cannot progress and its welfare will be in jeopardy.

Peace is the characteristic of the mind of Man. That is the innate quality of the mind. In order to search for Peace, there is no need to go anywhere else. As gold and silver lie hidden under the Earth and pearl and coral under the sea, Peace and Joy also lie hidden in the activities of the Mind. Desirous of acquiring these hidden treasures, if one dives and turns mental activities inward, then he becomes full of Prema or Love. Only those, who have so filled themselves with Love and who live in the light of that Love, can be called Men.

Life is a long journey through time and religion confers peace for the present and encouragement for the future. We must believe that we are at present undergoing the consequences of our own activities in the past.

It is a great source of peace that people can be content with their present conditions, because they know they themselves were the cause and know that if one does good and meritorious deeds now, it is possible to build a happy future.

In this world, there are several branches of learning, like physics, music, literature, and mathematics. Of all these forms of knowledge, Self Knowledge is sovereign. Without its attainment, one cannot enjoy any peace. Though one may gain renown and recognition in the world, one will not experience happiness without Self-knowledge. "Knowledge of the Soul," "Knowledge of God," and "Spiritual Knowledge" - all these expressions connote that wisdom, which promotes full awareness of soul and God. Self-knowledge is that knowledge, which by acquiring it, everything else is known. A person with self-knowledge can indeed be acclaimed as all-knowing.

Sacrifice is sweeter than enjoyment. Sacrifice should become the aim of life. Only through sacrifice can one attain peace. Sorrows do not flee from us as long as the mind is not at peace with itself. Agonies dwell forever within us. Without the tranquillity of the soul, any amount of wealth cannot be of any use. Surrendering the fruits of action with a dispassionate mind is eligible to be termed sacrifice. Purity of mind alone can confer upon it tranquillity.

In this era of technology, it is becoming increasingly difficult to lead peaceful lives. Men are becoming the targets of various types of mental ailments. In countries on the frontline of civilisation, like America and England, people have lost the delight of natural sleep at night. They experience only artificial sleep induced by the tablets they swallow. As a consequence of these and many other drugs taken to ward off other ills, they suffer more and more from diseases of the heart and blood pressure. In the end, they render themselves unhealthy. Such lives are highly artificial. People have sunk into fear and anxiety; mentally on one side and physically on the other, they have no rest. Drugs, tablets, capsules, and pills are produced in millions, but the general health has not improved. Besides, these new types of illness have emerged and are developing fast. A few intelligent Westerners have realised that their only refuge is Yoga; they have confirmed their conclusion by means of experiments; they have taken to Yoga with increasing faith.

Man, too, can transform himself through self-effort and discrimination from his present status. The moral forces permeating the cosmos will certainly promote our achievement. But, man is too immersed in the all-pervasive delusion to take advantage of these and elevate himself. He is not aware of the path of peace and harmony in the world. He is not able to hold on to the good and avoid the bad. He cannot establish himself in the Righteousness Path.

All religious dogmas, except a few, can easily be harmonised and reconciled. The same God is being extolled and adored under various names, through varied ceremonial rituals, in the many religions of man. In every age, for every race and community of peoples, God has sent Prophets to establish peace and goodwill. Since, at the present time, many religions have spread worldwide, they have lost fraternal feelings and have suffered in validity, thereby. There is an urgent need for harmony.

Turn the mind away from the sensory world through the practice of discrimination and non-attachment. Then, you attain the no-mind experience. Well, you have to remember another thing: trying to control the mind, without a clear understanding of the nature of the sensory world is a vain, valueless effort. The attachment will not end. The agitation will not cease so easily.

To know that the Soul, which is the goal of realisation, is devoid of sleep, birth, name, form, and so on, that it is eternally Self-effulgent, to know this is to transcend all agitation of the mind. Attempting to curb the mind without the aid of discrimination or to make known to man the unreality of subject-object relationship is like the attempt to empty the ocean by means of a blade of grass, foolish and fruitless. Be firmly fixed in the conviction that the world is a myth and then, you can aspire for Peace and Fearlessness.

In fact, the desire to know God, to love God, and be loved by God is not a desire, which binds. When awareness of God dawns in all its splendour, every worldly, sensual desire is reduced to ashes in the flames of that Awareness. The individual self will turn towards the Universal Self as soon as desire comes to an end, and it will delight in supreme Peace. The self must break off all contact with the non-self, so that it can earn immortality.

Prompted by the urge to advance the progress of others, when a person dedicates his wealth, skill, and intelligence, his position and status, he becomes truly great. Such a one is the purposeful seer for the world. He fulfils unfailingly the vow of sefless service. He, who is conscious of his basic duties and obligations, and spends his days in carrying them out in practice, will be in supreme peace, wherever he may be. Through his influence, his neighbourhood too will share that peace.

Men have now become more vicious than ever. They utilise, much more than in past ages, their intelligence and skill to indulge in cruelty. Men relish and revel in inflicting pain on others, so much so that as history reveals, 15,000 wars have been waged during the last 5,500 years. There are no signs yet that this horrid pastime will terminate! The impending atomic war threatens to destroy the entire human race. What exactly is the cause of all this anxiety and fear? It is clear that the beast in man is still predominant. It has not yet been overcome. Only when this is achieved can we, our country, and the world attain peace and joy.

Man has to achieve many objects during his life. The highest and the most valuable of these is winning the Mercy of God, the Love of God. The love of God will add unto him the great wisdom he needs for attaining unshakable Inner Peace.

Every living being craves happiness; they do not long for misery. Some desire the acquisition of riches, some believe that gold can make them happy. Some amass articles of luxury, some collect vehicles, but everyone is set upon obtaining the things he believes can give him joy.

But, those, who know wherefrom they can obtain happiness, are very few in number.

Students require faith in themselves, more than most other qualities. The absence of self-confidence marks the beginning of one's decline. Today, the world is facing ruin and disaster, because people have lost confidence in themselves. Self-confidence alone is capable of granting peace and prosperity to each person. He receives good everywhere; he is honoured in all places. Whatever he touches becomes gold.

The Upanishads announce certain remedial spiritual practices to get rid of this obstacle to inner peace.

- The first practice is pranayama, Regulation of Breath. Pranayama is no gymnastics, nor a formidable exercise. The inhaling of air is Pooraka; the exhaling is Rechaka. Retention in between is Kumbhaka. The mind has to concentrate on the period of retention and on the processes of inhaling and exhaling. When attention is fixed thus, the inner talk on other irrelevant matters will end and mental strength is acquired.

- The second practice is immersion in karma, beneficial activity - that is to say, service to people, which will help diminish the ego sense, acts that are good and godly. When one's thoughts are engaged in such activities, the mind turns away from the talk it indulges in.

- Again, the practice of listening to spiritual advice, reflection on spiritual directions, discovering ways and means of confirming faith in the Spirit, recital of the names of God, and withdrawing the mind from sensual pursuits have been prescribed by the scriptures more for the silencing of this mental chatter, this inner talk, as a preparation for attaining the reality, than for its realisation.

Chapter - 13
Divine Discourse Of Bhagawan Sri Sathya Sai Baba

Date: 1st January, 2001; Occasion: New Year; Place: Prasanthi Nilayam

There is pain in pleasure also; none can separate them. It is pain that leads to pleasure. In fact, both pain and pleasure are the effects of the Kali Age. (Telugu Poem)

Embodiments of Love! Years have rolled by, but man has not developed noble feelings. A true human being is one with a good mind. The qualities of a good mind are: it has the brightness of the sun and coolness of the moon; it makes one utter sacred words and confers peace on the society. One with compassion, love, forbearance, sympathy, and sacred qualities has become scarce. How can one bereft of human qualities be called a human being?

Man has originated from Nature. Earth sustains life. Sun gives light. Trees give oxygen. Water quenches our thirst and air helps us to live. How is it that man, born out of the five elements and sustained by them, does not possess the sacred qualities of the five elements? Having been born out of and brought up by Nature, man should practise and propagate the ideals set by Nature. Birds, animals, and trees follow Nature and lead an ideal life. Trees inhale the poisonous carbon dioxide and exhale the life-supporting oxygen. Even the animals discharge their duties and help man in many ways. But, having been born as a human being, why is it that man is not practising human values? He is not in a position to practise and propagate human values in society, as he himself has lost them.

Embodiments Of Love!

Every man expects the New Year to confer on him peace, happiness, and prosperity. New Year does not bring happiness or sorrow with it. Yesterday is the same as today and today is the same as tomorrow. Days are the same, but one experiences either pleasure, or pain, depending on one's own actions. Meritorious deeds will not confer misery and sinful deeds cannot give happiness. One is bound to face the consequences of one's actions. But, one treats pleasure and pain alike, when one becomes the recipient of God's grace. God's grace destroys mountains of sins and confers peace. But, due to the impact of Kali Age, man has lost faith in God. He is after money and power. How can such a person attain Divinity? Man can rise from the level of the human to the Divine, only by practising human values.

Years come and go, so also pleasure and pain. Nothing confers permanent bliss, except the experience of the Atma. Man cannot attain peace and happiness from his actions, unless he has sacred feelings within. Many people expect the New Year to confer happiness and prosperity on them. But, in fact, New Year only confers on you the results of your past actions. In order to atone for your past sins, you have to cultivate sacred qualities and involve yourself in sacred activities more and more, in the New Year. In fact, Bliss is within you, it originates from your sacred feelings. So, you have to manifest bliss from within - it cannot be bestowed on you by others. None can take away the bliss from you and you cannot obtain it from outside.

The heart is the centre of sacred feelings. It is filled with compassion. It is compassion that gives rise to sacred feelings. One has to develop compassion, spread the light of love, and cultivate Divine feelings. Without doing so, how can one expect Time to confer happiness on him? One gets what one does. If one expects good results, one must cultivate good feelings. With purity of heart, steadiness of mind, and selfless actions, one can become the recipient of Divine Grace, which will remove any amount of sufferings in a trice. One cannot achieve anything without Divine Grace. So, one has to undertake such activities, which will confer Divine Grace. Peace and happiness cannot be obtained from the external world. Only through Divine Grace can one be peaceful and happy. People celebrate the advent of the New Year with singing and dancing. That enthusiasm and happiness are but momentary. What man needs is permanent peace and happiness. How can he expect to attain permanent happiness by indulging in worldly deeds? He has to undertake sacred activities in order to attain permanent happiness.

Embodiments Of Love!

Under all circumstances, let your feelings be pure and ideal. Let all your actions be for the welfare of others. The Vedas declare: Paropakaaraya Punyaya Paapaaya Parapeedanam (One attains merit by serving others and commits sin by hurting them). When your feelings are sacred, you will get sacred results without your asking. Due to the impact of Kali Age, man's thought, words, and deeds are not in harmony with each other. You may say or do anything - the result you get depends on your feelings. So, make your feelings sacred and become a good human being. One with good feelings and good mind alone can be called a good human being.

Sometimes, deeds done with good mind may yield bad results. The result may appear adverse, but there is goodness latent in it. A good mind will never change, because of such results. Man is essentially good. So, he ought to lead a life of goodness. But, today, man wavers every moment. It is due to lack of Will Power. Man should have unwavering mind and steady vision. Then, he will not be subjected to any hardships. Only God's Grace can help man overcome these negative tendencies.

One may be a millionaire, but his wealth will not redeem him, if his feelings are impure. Even if a man does not possess anything, he can still achieve the highest, if he has purity of heart. Anything that a man of purity sees or touches turns into gold. On the other hand, if he lacks purity and effort in the right direction, even a stick in his hand will turn into a snake. Sankalpamoolam Idam Jagat (Thoughts form the basis of the entire world). Some people feel their expectations are not fructifying in spite of their best efforts. This is mainly due to absence of purity in their feelings and intentions.

Today marks the commencement of the New Year, 2001. Next year, it will become 2002. Destiny does not change with the change in year. Along with the change in year, your actions, too, should change for the better. Only then, you will get good results.

Students!

You will fare well in the examination, only when you work hard throughout the year. As is the feeling, so is the action. As is the action, so is the result. Sometimes, you may question the adverse outcome of a good action. But, in fact, good actions will never yield bad results. Bad result implies an element of negativity in the intentions. It is a human weakness to see only the good in oneself, ignoring the bad.

"Pleasure and pain, good and bad co-exist, none can separate them. You cannot find pleasure or pain, good or bad to the exclusion of the other. Pleasure results, when difficulties fructify." (Telugu Poem)

Even a sweet mango tastes sour, when it is plucked prematurely. It should be allowed to ripen. Only then, it will taste sweet. So, do not get disheartened, if your actions do not yield the desired results immediately. Your efforts are bound to fructify in due course of time.

Embodiments Of Love!

You have been waiting for the commencement of the New Year, with great expectations. Your efforts must be in accordance with the expectation. Before undertaking any activity, you should discriminate and enquire into the pros and cons. Today, man has lost the sense of discrimination. He does not know how to respect and behave among elders. He should make proper use of the Mathi (mind), Gathi (destiny), Stithi (position), and Sampatthi (wealth) that God has bestowed on him. The six evil traits of man, viz. desire, anger, greed, infatuation, pride, and jealousy arise due to the defects in his food and habits. Food and habits are responsible for the qualities in man, good or bad.

The sacred qualities that originate from the heart are true and eternal. They correspond to the inward path (Nivritti), whereas all the worldly tendencies, like amassing wealth, taking up jobs, playing games, desiring for positions of authority, etc., correspond to the outward path (Pravritti). Worldly tendencies originate from the head and are bound to change. Only the inward tendencies that originate from the heart are true and eternal. Ignoring the inward tendencies, man takes to the outward path. Consequently, he is unable to attain permanent happiness. He treads the path of Pravritti, but expects the results corresponding to Nivritti. All that he sees, says, and does have become polluted with untruth and unrighteousness. In fact, his entire life has become Pravritti-oriented. He should give up the outward path and direct his vision inward. Before entertaining any thought, he should discriminate whether it is good or bad. One, who follows the outward path, can never attain permanent happiness, getting frustrated or restless. For example, you may be 20 years old or 40 years old. You have been eating food everyday, all these years. But, can your hunger ever be satisfied permanently? No. Only the taste varies, but hunger is the same for everybody.

> *Food may vary, but hunger is the same,*
> *Jewels are many, but gold is the same,*
> *The colour of the cows may vary, but milk is the same,*
> *Forms are many, but God is one,*
> *Beings are many, but breath is one. (Telugu Poem)*

Man leads a life of delusion, because he sees diversity in unity. He faces many hardships to carry on with the sojourn of his life. But, life is transient. To lead such an ephemeral life, why should one take to the wrong path and get deluded? So long as one is alive, one should tread the path of truth and set an ideal. Only then can one's life be sanctified. Truthful activities alone can confer eternal peace.

A poet composes many verses in praise of God. He extols God grandiloquently and ultimately, prays for His protection. The feeling is important and not the manner, in which the verses are composed. One may extol God, according to one's own capacity, but one should do so with pure, steady, and sacred feelings. One may be doing Bhajan, offering worship, and undertaking service activities for a number of years. But, all this will prove futile, if there is no transformation of the heart. Heart should be filled with compassion. Only then can it be called a temple of God. Otherwise, it becomes verily a devil's den.

The New Year does not bring anything new with it. The day, when fresh and sacred thoughts originate in your heart, is the real New Year day. As you all consider this day as New Year day and welcome it with enthusiasm, I bless you all, so that you may cultivate fresh, sacred, and ideal feelings. I desire that you share with others all that you consider as good. I want you lead a peaceful and blissful life and become role models for the rest of the country.

At times, evil qualities, like desire, anger, and hatred, may arise in you, but they should not be allowed to enter the mind. Once they are refused permission, they will automatically withdraw. If they are allowed to enter the mind, they will remain in it. A small example. When someone comes to your doorstep with his baggage, if you receive him and start exchanging pleasantries, he will immediately enter and settle down in your house. On the other hand, if you ignore him completely, he will go to a hotel or a lodge. Likewise, when the evil qualities try to enter your mind, just ignore them. Then, they will go back to the place of their origin. On the other hand, if you entertain them, they will rule over you. When you come across something evil, do not look at it, talk about it, or listen to it. Just ignore it. That is the true human quality.

You will allow only your friends and relatives to enter your house through the main doors. Will anyone allow the donkeys and pigs to enter the house, just because it has doors? Your body has got nine doors. You should permit through them only that, which is sacred. Do not allow the evil to enter. Only then can you attain peace.

Human life is highly noble, valuable, and divine! Do not put it to misuse, by giving room to evil qualities. Use the power of discrimination and make proper use of the senses. Only then will your life be redeemed. You will attain immortality and infinite bliss. Start a novel and Divine life in this new year. Give up all the old, unsacred feelings. Cultivate divine feelings. Once you have divine feelings, no other feeling can enter your mind. Install God within, then peace will automatically follow.

Embodiments Of Love!

I bless you all, so that you may lead your lives with peace, prosperity, and happiness.

Appendix A
Passage To India

By absolute coincidence, I bought Dr. Mohammed Sadek Aladawy's book about *Spiritual Therapy Between Science And Application*, in which he mentioned on one of its pages that there are some contemporary cases, nowadays, which prove man's coming back from the world of spirits to re-exist on Earth (reincarnation).

And one of the renowned cases today, on the world level, is an Indian spiritual master, known by the name 'Sai Baba'.

Since I was busy at the time, I actually forgot his book's subject and after one year, I received from one of the Western publishers book lists about spiritualism. I halted at a page including some twenty books about Sai Baba. I remembered where I had previously come upon His name and I selected from that list two books, one of which is titled *Sai Baba: The Ultimate Experience*, by Phyllis Krystal and the other book titled *Walking The Path With Sai Baba*, authored by the Australian journalist Howard Murphet. I then sent in a request for these two books and upon their receipt, I read them in-depth with much interest. Upon completion of reading about this legendary personality, I felt a strong desire to meet this person, 'Sai Baba' the great spiritual master.

Next, I visited the Indian Cultural Centre in Cairo and met with Dr. Ihsan Rahman, the Indian Cultural Adviser and asked him about Sai Baba and whether He was still alive, to which he informed me that He had died a while ago and he then let me know about a Yoga course held at the Indian Cultural Centre, in which I promptly subscribed. In the first Yoga course day, I met with Dr. Praphakar, a Yoga instructor, who had just come from India and asked him about Sai Baba, and he informed me that there are two personalities in Sai Baba; the first personality, which died a long time ago, and the second personality, which is still alive. I felt glad about this news and looked forward to meeting that miraculous man. I wished fervently from the depths of my soul that Sai Baba would disclose to me a prophecy.

After a few weeks following this wish, during my attendance in a scientific conference, I happened to coincidentally sit beside an Indian scholar, named Dr. Niela Kanta. This was the first time he travelled out of India. Upon chatting with him, I learned that he was an old solicitor of Sai Baba's, the preacher of the great generosities, and that he would be able to help me locate Him in Brindavan. He then invited me to attend a world conference to be held in India, where he could facilitate my meeting Sai Baba. I accepted his invitation. I travelled to India in March, 1996 and on the day of my trip, I suffered acute back pain, which I tried to reduce by taking some pain killers, insisting on proceeding with my trip whatever the prevailing circumstances. I arrived in Mumbai and reached Chennai to attend the scientific conference, meeting with Dr. Niela Kanta, who then guided me to Sai Baba's domicile in Brindavan, near the famous city of Bengaluru.

Then, suddenly, a dream became a reality. I sat within the rows of thousands of squatting people, awaiting the presence of the great spiritual instructor. While I was still suffering pain in my lower back and after two hours of waiting, and repetitions of religious psalms, Sai Baba made His appearance, walking among the attendants' rows. As He approached me, the fatigue and exhaustion in my body disappeared, feeling an unusual energy penetrating my whole body and even my back pain had suddenly disappeared.

On the closing day, I attended once more, carrying a letter, in which I described some wishes wherein I requested the blessings of Sai Baba to be fulfilled. I learned that if he takes the letter, this becomes a grand prophecy. Sai Baba made His appearance, crossed the attendants' rows, where I was luckily sitting, and He picked up my letter. I then saw Him before me, lifting His empty hand near me and materialising from it ashes in the form of a cone upon one of the attendants' head, as though I was watching a science fiction movie. Then, Sai Baba proceeded forward, where He took a seat before the attendants, who totalled about one hundred thousand and I noticed an illuminating halo about His head, ever expanding and enlarging. I was unable to believe my eyes. I properly discerned my vision and became sure of the fact of the existence of a shining halo, surrounding the great spiritual scholar's head.

One week after my return from India to Cairo, one of my two written wishes in the letter to Sai Baba was fulfilled. This wish was related to a personal problem, which persisted over three years without resolution; whereas the second wish, its symptoms began to appear.

Most important however, is the great prophecy of Sai Baba creating a deep-rooted *transformation* in my heart. My feelings towards God have become a focal point in my thoughts most of the time. This *transformation* is notable in spite of its being slow. In addition, my heart has become filled with love for all people and overflows with joy and happiness. Divine love has developed in the depths of my being and what a joyful feeling it is.

Dr. Abdelfattah M. Badawi

Appendix B
From Paris To Brindavan

Dr. Badawi and myself met some 5 years ago. Our relationship was only based on professional links. I discovered Sai Baba by reading books written by M. Coquet some 6 years ago. During my trip to Cairo in January, 1997, I was reading J. Roof's book *Pathways To God* and was very interested in its message, which I felt in complete accordance with my inner being. When Dr. Badawi and myself were concluding our meeting one evening, in the hotel where I stayed, I felt my inner voice telling me to speak about my readings and I could hear myself talking about Sai Baba.

It was a big surprise to discover that Dr. A. Badawi not only knew Sai Baba, but also was a devotee and had the chance to travel to India to see Him. He introduced his project to write a book in Arabic and to travel to Puttaparthi, to submit the manuscript and get Sai Baba's blessings. Since Dr. Badawi has a good friend in India, the travel details could easily be arranged and I was invited to seriously consider to travel with him to India and visit Sai Baba's ashram. Since my first discovery of Sai Baba, I had, of course, always been willing to meet the Avatar. But, I was planning to organise this trip sometime in the future, when my professional and private life would allow me some free time. I was also convinced that meeting such a personality requires a long spiritual preparation. In such a mood, I merely answered the invitation with a 'why not'.

Things turned out going much faster than expected and his friend Shreeram in India proposed to travel during September, because the climatic conditions are very good during that season in Puttaparthi. I could not give my approval to this trip on the spot, since I have to arrange my visa, ticket, and permission to take a vacation. This could have been difficult, because I spent most of my time in Morocco, where the company I am working for is based. In France, the Indian Embassy, where I would apply for the visa, is in Paris. To make a long story short, I had everything ready for the trip to India in a matter of 2 weeks. Unfortunately, when I called Dr. Badawi for the final arrangement to meet in Mumbai, he told me that he would not travel due to a very serious backache, which forced him to stay lying in bed. Although I felt very sorry, I did have a choice to change my flight reservations and decided to proceed alone.

Since the day I knew I was travelling, I prayed to receive assistance from **Sai Baba**, for helping me as a Westerner to accommodate with the way of living in the ashram. My heart was full with happiness and I was very confident that this trip would change my life.

Despite the late arrival at Mumbai, Shreeram was awaiting me and gave full assistance to reach the hotel, where he had booked a room for me. The following day, we flew from Mumbai to Bengaluru, where a taxi was waiting to take us to Puttaparthi. When we reached the ashram, it was not difficult to find an accommodation and to be ready for the afternoon Darshan. Shreeram, unfortunately, had to travel the same way back to Mumbai, since he was going on a business trip the following day.

So, in a matter of weeks, the dream turned to be a reality and I was ready to see Sai Baba in person. The first thing I was planning to do was to write a letter to Sai Baba, asking to give His blessings to Dr. Badawi, who was working on a book in Arabic to spread His message in the Arabic speaking countries. That was what I did and I was very happy to see Sai Baba coming to my place to take this letter, when I offered it to Him in the first attempt. My roommate told me that this was great luck and a very good sign. But, my first impression was a great disappointment, because I was expecting something very strong and in a way, supernatural. This was not the case at all and when I saw Sai Baba coming to give His Darshan so close to me, I did not feel anything special. It was actually the opposite and I was very puzzled to imagine that this little body, dressed in His orange robe, was an incarnation of God Himself with all the related characteristics of the Avatar: omniscient, omnipresent, and omnipotent. Although being in the ashram was a very good experience, I was wondering what I will gain to be here, since everytime I saw Sai Baba, nothing moved me. I was always lucky to be seated in the first row of persons and had the chance to see Him materialising the Vibhuti from thin air, and distribute it to the people, who were so happy to receive the holy ashes. This situation lasted for 3 days and I was so disappointed that I decided to write a letter to Sai Baba, asking for some kind of assistance.

Having written my worries, I was happy to see Baba taking my letter during the next Darshan. The following morning, when I was quietly sitting among many people, but in the first row, Baba was coming very close and looked at me with His lovely glance. My heart jumped in my chest and I felt a kind of loving energy, which I had never experienced before. This was Baba's answer to my request. After Darshan, I had to remain seated for meditation and to avoid this loving energy being dispersed by early movement.

What I learnt from this experience is that being close to Baba is important, because in His presence, physical, spiritual, emotional levels can be ***transformed***.

But, most important is to look for Him inside our heart and recognise the divinity in every being, human, animal, plant, or mineral. This is not easy at all, but with time, if our heart is open, this will happen and bring a great happiness.

"Love All. Serve All," this is what we have to attend to and Baba is helping us reach the goal.

Mr. Jean-Paul Ducotterd

Appendix C
A Journey To Sai Baba. The Interview

"Sham El Nessim", which coincided with the 1st of May, 2000, was a day celebrated by the ancient Egyptians. It represented for them the beginning of spring. The day Mother Earth starts its rebirthing process. On that day, we, as a small group of Egyptian devotees, were granted an interview by Swami. We were a group of four ladies, which made Swami exclaim, "No men, only ladies... good." We were led into the interview room with a Malaysian couple, an Indian lady, and a Canadian lady.

As we all sat on the floor, Swami noticed that the Malaysian gentleman was wearing a diamond ring with one stone missing. He took the ring, blew on it, and then before our eyes, the missing stone was replaced. He then materialised in front of us a plastic sachet with medicinal pills and told him to take it. Swami then turned His attention to the Canadian lady, whom He apparently knew and materialised for her a beautiful golden chain with a pendant, containing Baba's picture surrounded with diamonds. He then looked at her fingers and asked, "What ring is that?" to which she answered, "Swami, You gave it to me last year," and He said, "No good," and materialised a much finer one. He then looked at us and gave each one some vibhuti in our hands, whitish in colour and crystal like in taste, and tapped us on our heads while asking and repeating our names. One of us had a Koran in her hands. He looked at it and said, "Allah Akbar, God is one, many religions but one God, many trees but one Earth, many stars but one sky." He then took us in a smaller private room and talked to each one of us, having complete knowledge of our lives. We observed over His head a huge, free halo of a very bright colour. After talking to us, we went back into the main room, where the Malaysian gentleman asked Swami to sign Swami's picture, whereupon Swami said, "Treat picture like God, but not God like picture." He then blessed us all and ended the interview.

For us four, it was as if we were in a dream, not really absorbing what we saw. We felt peace and happiness and knew that Swami represents real truth and love. Our lives changed from that day on. For us, it was as if we were reborn and went through a transformation on that day - "Sham El Nassim" day.

Mrs. Randa El Massry

Appendix D
A Journey To Self-Peace

I invited "Dr. Sayed Nassar" - the big surgeon - to travel with me to India and to visit Sai Baba, as I visited Him four times before and this visit would be the fifth. I wrote a book in Arabic before about Sai Baba, called *Divine Love*, and this time, I had finished writing a book in English about Him, called *A Journey To Self Peace*. The purpose of my visit this time was to let Sai Baba bless this book, before printing and publishing it. There were a group of Egyptians composed of five women and one dentist, who intended to visit Sai Baba in the same period.

Searching for self-peace and to know the places, in which spirituals could be practised, I decided to travel with Dr. Nassar, his daughter Nefertiti, and his son Ani, an engineer, as both of them were concerned with spirituality and its applications.

Saturday, March 10th, 2001

We travelled from Cairo to Mumbai by plane and arrived in Mumbai in the afternoon. We decided to stay in one of Mumbai's hotels.

Sunday, March 11th

We went to Bengaluru by plane, in the morning. It took about one hour and a quarter. In Bengaluru Airport, we asked about the current residence of Sai Baba, as He was moving among three residences. In this period, He was in Puttaparthi Village as it was His place of birth & home, and this was a small village in a very underdeveloped area, in Andhra Pradesh state. Now, it has become a developed spiritual centre for education and health, and it is called Prasanthi Nilayam, which meant abode of peace. It became a town now.

We took an air-conditioned car and went to Puttaparthi, and after having a round for about 3 hours in the Indian countryside, we arrived at Sai Baba's residence and at the town entrance, we found a big carving with beautiful, bright colours, in which was written in English that Duty is God and Work is Worship.

Sai Baba's residence was called Ashram. It was a town that had all services of residence, restaurants, supermarkets, bakery, shops for selling fruits and vegetables, bank, communications, post office, telephone and fax, lecturers' hall and library. The most important place in this town is called Prasanthi Mandir, which meant Prayer Hall. The hall was for praying and singing religious songs, this is a very luxurious building of Indian architectural style with beautiful, bright colours, which was decorated with paintings, statues, and marble shafts, blue and gold ceiling with a big number of Crystal Lamps. This place was wide enough to take twenty two thousand visitors. The wide, luxurious worshipping hall was annexed to a place for Sai Baba to meet His devotees and visitors, to talk and sing religious songs, and there were small rooms for meeting foreign guests. In this town, there were wide rooms to take hundreds of the Indian poor visitors, in which they were sleeping on the floor, each room was annexed to a public toilet. Some of these rooms were for men and others for women and children. There were buildings, in which the rich visitors stayed. Some of these buildings were for Indian visitors and others were for foreign ones. There were four layers in each building. Each layer was divided into separate rooms and each room had its bathroom. The furniture was very simple - 2 beds, 2 plastic chairs, and a table. There was no air-conditioning, except ceiling fan, in spite of the high temperature, which was between 32°C and 45°C during the whole year.

The poor visitors used to take coupons to have their meals in a special restaurant. But, the rich visitors were accustomed to pay the price of residence and food, as there was an Indian restaurant as well as a Western one with lower prices. The residence in the room cost 100 rupees per night, which was about two dollars or eight Egyptian pounds. The meal cost about two Egyptian pounds. All the food was vegetarian and there was no meat. We went to an office for the foreign visitors and after registering our names, they gave us two rooms for residence; one for Dr. Nassar and his daughter, and the other for me and Any, Dr. Nassar's son. This was according to the instructions of the administration that only two persons were to stay in each room.

Dr. Nassar took his Arabic book draft, which was about the modern spiritual science, after finishing it in handwriting, hoping that Sai Baba might see and bless it. Also, he made a portrait for Sai Baba with oil colours, in order to give it to Him as a gift in his first visit to Him.

We found that there were a great number of foreign visitors coming from different countries, such as USA, England, France, Switzerland, Russia, Germany, Belgium, Italy, Spain, Turkey, and Iran, as well as from Latin American countries, like Venezuela, Argentina, and others, in addition to the Indian people of upper, middle, and lower classes.

The daily programme in the Ashram began at 5 a.m., when the bell rang for the first time, so that visitors could enter the worshipping hall in a quiet and organised way. Those, who would attend early, would have the opportunity of sitting in the first row. All the people were entering this hall without shoes or slippers. All the people were searched accurately, by sevadals, and they were not allowed to have anything except a book and a pillow to sit on, as all the visitors were sitting on the floor. There were some chairs in the sides of the hall for the patients and the handicapped persons. After twenty minutes, the bell rang for the second time. Then, it rang for the third time in order to begin with what was called Omkar, in which thousands of people began to make some sounds in a low voice. Then, they began to raise their voices and then, they lowered their voices again, and this was repeated 21 times. Then, they uttered the word 'Shanthi' three times, which meant peace. A group of men began to sing some religious songs inside the worshipping hall. Then, they went outside, turned around the building, and they returned to the hall. After that, some women began to sing another religious song, accompanied by beating drums and some musical instruments, doing what the group of men had done.

At 6 a.m., all the people would be sitting on the floor in complete silence, waiting for Sai Baba, the Master. They called him 'Swami', which meant consecrated man. At about half past six, the ceremony of 'Darshan' or seeing the Master began with playing soft music, when Sai Baba went out of His house, which was near the worshipping hall and walked slowly on a red carpet, wearing an orange robe that covered all His body, bare-footed, and having black, heavy hair. He passed by women first and then, by the men. While He was walking, He looked to the right and left sides and smiled, stretching His right hand to collect some of the letters and messages from those, who wanted His help and His blessings to solve their problems. Then, He put these letters in His left hand.

From time to time, He used to speak to some people and sometimes, chose one of them to attend an interview. Fifteen minutes later, the ceremony of 'Darshan' would end. Seeing the Master meant receiving the good and holy qualities and the energy, which would help those, who had seen Him, to purify themselves and their conscience. Everyone, who saw Him, would like to keep this fast look of the Master, as if it were a divine look. After that, Sai Baba went to His private room in order to meet those, whom He had chosen. He talked to them, giving them some advice, answered their questions, and did some miraculous things before them. At 9 a.m., the ceremony of what was called 'Bhajans', which were devotional songs, began. At that time, Sai Baba sat beside His devotees, who were singing some religious songs. The meeting was attended by the school students in order to meet the Master and to participate in these songs.

This ceremony lasted for half an hour. The ceremonies of 'Darshan' and 'Bhajan' were repeated again, at half past two, with the same order, but in the afternoon, it was allowed for the foreign visitors to enter a special room, 'Mandir', and to sit with Sai Baba in meditation for about fifteen minutes.

Monday Dawn, March 12th

At dawn, we sat with men in the second row, while Dr. Nassar's daughter was sitting with women in the ninth row. The men sat on a side, while the women were sitting on the other side of the worshipping hall. And as usual, Sai Baba appeared while soft music was played. He walked slowly, collecting some of the letters and not all of them, as He chooses what He wanted. He stopped in front of an Indian person, moved His right hand, and put some of the vibhuti in his hand and in the hand of the person sitting beside him. When He came to our place, we stretched our hands to give Him our letters, some of which were personal and the others were of our friends. All of these letters were of patients, who needed help for recovery. Sai Baba, unfortunately, looked at us and didn't take letters, going towards the other side.

We began to feel disappointed as Sai Baba was so near us, looking at us, and when we stretched our hands to give Him our letters, He turned to the other side, as if He were telling us not to be in a hurry and as if saying that there were many others, who came before you and were in need of My help.

We had to go to the lecturers' room to attend a lecture about Sai Baba's mission and about the residence in Ashram. The new coming visitors have to attend this lecture in order to be able to continue staying in this place and the one, who was giving the lecture, was a very nice person.

After the lecture had finished, Dr. Nassar thanked the lecturer, asking him about the vegetarian food and if it was possible to eat fish and eggs. The lecturer answered him, saying that there were degrees to become vegetarian. It was better not to eat fish, even eggs, as there might be an embryo inside this egg and by eating it, you would kill this embryo. So, you could start, from now, to eat vegetables, fruits, and milk only. Dr. Nassar told him about what happened with Sai Baba and that He didn't take the letters from us, although He was so near us. The lecturer told him not to worry, while he was smiling, saying that Sai

Baba would take the letters from us, as He knew everything and everyone, who came to the Ashram, and why he came. Sai Baba offered help to everyone in need of Him. Dr. Nassar said that he had a portrait of Sai Baba and asked how he could present it to Him, while they prevent the visitors from taking anything with them in the worshipping hall. The lecturer told him to send it to Swami by mail, as He used to receive all the letters sent to Him by mail. His speech relieved us and enabled us to regain hope after feeling so disappointed. In the afternoon, we went to attend 'Darshan' ceremony and we took the letters with us, but in vain.

Tuesday, March 13th

We went early at dawn to sit in the first row, but at that time, we sat in the third row. The ceremony of 'Darshan' began. Sai Baba appeared, walking slowly among His visitors till He came near us. He looked at us and smiled. Then, He took the letters from me and from Dr. Nassar, but Ani wasn't able to give Him his letters, as Sai Baba turned to the other side.

We felt happy as Sai Baba took the letters from us and began to have hope.

Among Dr. Nassar's letters, there was a personal letter, in which he mentioned the following points:

1. He believed in spirituality, since he was young and now, he tried to establish an Egyptian association for spiritual studies and that he was in need of Sai Baba's help in this respect.

2. He had finished writing his book on new spiritualism for the Arab readers and he wished Sai Baba to bless it.

3. He had painted an oil portrait of Him, wishing that Sai Baba might accept it as a gift for Him.

4. He was thanking God for his good financial situation, but he wished to have good health in order to continue his spiritual studies.

After the end of the ceremony of Darshan and having taken breakfast, we went out of the Ashram in order to cover the portrait to send it to Sai Baba by mail, after writing His name and address on the cover.

Nefertiti was not able to give her letters to Sai Baba on this day, but an inner voice told her, "Neither today, nor tomorrow, but after that." She asked about the explanation of this inspiration. Her father told her that it was clear that Sai Baba would not meet us, neither on Monday, nor on Tuesday. It might be after that and he advised her to give her letters to her brother Ani, as he had a greater opportunity to give his letters to Sai Baba. After Sai Baba had taken the letters from us, Dr. Nassar was hoping that he would meet Sai Baba on Thursday, after the arrival of the rest of the group from Egypt.

Wednesday, March 14th

After attending Darshan and having breakfast, Dr. Nassar went to visit the hospital, which was about five kilometres from the Ashram, as one of his friends, who was called Sudheer, a businessman, asked him to visit the manager of the hospital and he sent his brother to accompany him on this visit.

The manager of the hospital received Dr. Nassar in his office, with great hospitality. The hospital manager began to explain to Dr. Nassar Sai Baba's philosophy and his work, saying that he was concerned with education as he established schools for all stages of education till the university. This was a full, board school, where they were learning the academic sciences, as well as moral values in order to become good citizens.

Sai Baba was concerned with health as He decided to establish this hospital on His birthday, in 1991. The area of the land, on which the hospital was established, is 100 acres. The hospital was surrounded with gardens full of trees and flowers. The hospital was of the Indian architectural style with its bright colours and high domes. There were

300 beds in this hospital, which was called 'Sri Sathya Sai Institute Of Higher Medical Sciences', in which open heart operations, urinary passage operations, kidney transfer, lithotrity, as well as macrophathalmia operations, and treating with Laser were currently conducted. This hospital was established for treating all patients for free. Patients all over India, even outside it, come for treatment in this hospital. There was a big waiting list. After that, Sai Baba was concerned about water as water meant life. He made a big project for providing drinkable water in the region. The hospital manager sent one of the doctors with Dr. Nassar, in order to have a round in the hospital to see all the hospital departments, the various labs, radiology, and sterilisation departments. He has seen also the operation rooms, which were highly equipped with the newest medical equipment.

Dr. Nassar saw the patients' rooms and some cases of different ages that conducted open heart operations. The hospital is really of a very high standard. On Wednesday afternoon, the four Egyptian women arrived, who were Dr. Magda, Professor of Ophthalmology in the Faculty of Medicine, Cairo University, Mrs. Laila, Mrs. Randa, and Mrs. Janen, who was a Swiss spouse of an Egyptian and they were accompanied by Dr. Wadie Barsoum, a dentist. A woman, called Silivi, would come after 2 days. In this way, the number of the Egyptian group would be nine persons (five women and four men).

Thursday, March 15th

We attended the ceremony 'Darshan' and as usual, the Egyptian men were sitting on one side, while the Egyptian women were sitting on the other side, wearing a green scarf, in which there was a white star and full moon as well as the word 'Egypt'. So, it would be easy to know each other among the great number of people. At about a quarter to six, Sai Baba appeared while some soft music was played and He began to collect the letters, and He came near us as Ani, Dr. Wadie and I were sitting in the first row, while Dr. Nassar was sitting in the fourth row on the other side. Sai Baba took the letters from Ani and He saw my book on my leg and His picture on the cover. He touched my head with His blessed hand. After that, He came near Dr. Wadie, who told Him, "Interview, Sai Baba." Sai Baba smiled and said, "How many are you?" I and Ani answered him at the same time, saying, "Nine." He said, "Go." The sevadals showed us the way to a place in front of Sai Baba's private room and the Egyptian women joined us, as one of the Indian sevadals guided them on the way, and we sat in front of the room, waiting for Sai Baba. After passing among the great number of people, Sai Baba came to us and He looked at Ani, asking him, "When will you travel?" Ani answered, "Next day." (Nobody mentioned the date of departure, but He knew that we would travel the next day. So, He allowed us to meet Him as we were about to leave."

Sai Baba led us to His private room. It was a small room, which was not more than 3 x 3 metres. There was a turning chair covered with red plush in one of the corners of the room. We found a woman from Belgium and her husband, and a young man of about twenty years old coming from Argentina. All of us sat on the floor in a circle. The men were on His right side and the women on His left side. He went to turn on the fan, because of the high temperature, as there was no air-conditioner in the room. Then, He sat and welcomed us. He asked Dr. Magda about the half moon and the star drawn on the scarf. She said that it was the previous flag of Egypt. Then, He smiled and said, "Mohammed."

Then, He looked to the woman coming from Belgium, asking her about the computer. She smiled and talked to her husband for a short time. Sai Baba stood up, moving His right hand so that the ash would be materialised, which is called Vibhuti. He put a little of it in the hand of each woman and He threw the rest of it on the floor. All the women swallowed this dust. Then, He returned to His chair. Looking to the Belgium woman, He moved His right hand in a round move, so a necklace of gold and precious stones fell out of His hand. He asked her to bow her head in order to let Him put the necklace around her neck. So, she bowed and accepted the gift. Then, He looked at her and said that her husband would be jealous of her. After that, He looked at her husband, who was sitting next to Him, and found him wearing a ring made of gold and precious stones, on a finger in his left hand. He hit his hand softly and moved His right hand in a round move, so that a big watch made of gold fell out of His hand. Then, He looked at the woman, saying that she would be jealous of him. All of us laughed. The husband stretched his hand to Sai Baba, after taking off his watch, to let Sai Baba put the new watch around his wrist. Then, he asked the wife about her husband's name. She said that his name is Gaupard Pierre and we found that the first letters of his name were written on the watch.

Then, Sai Baba stood up and asked us (the Egyptian group) to go with Him into another room; we went to the other room and sat on the floor in a circle, while Sai Baba sat on a turning chair. He asked Ani to turn on the fan. Ani went and turned it on. Sai Baba asked me a strange question, "How old are you?" I said, "Sixty five years old," and then, He asked me about His age and I said, "Seventy five." At that time, I remembered what I was thinking of while I was in Egypt, which was to ask Sai Baba when I would die. "Is seventy five the answer to my question?" I wondered in my mind. Sai Baba looked at me, took the book, and put it on His knees while He was looking at the cover. I explained the meaning of the cover. It was a portrait of Sai Baba, wearing white robe and beside Him, a mosque which He established in Puttaparthi and on the top of the mosque, there was a white pigeon. Sai Baba asked about this white pigeon. I told Him that my late father had drawn this pigeon and it represents peace. My book was written in English.

Sai Baba began to have a look upon the book. Then, He asked me to give Him a pen. He wrote on the first page, "With My blessings and love, Sai Baba."

I told Him that my first book in Arabic about Sai Baba, titled, 'Sai Baba and Divine Love Miracles' was severely criticised by the Egyptian newspaper. Sai Baba said that He knew that, but this was nuisance and not press. I told Sai Baba that I would publish my book in

USA and my coming book would be titled 'Sai Baba And Peace'. Sai Baba said, "You had to write about meanings and there was no need to mention names."

Then, Sai Baba looked at Dr. Nassar, asking him about his health. Before answering, He said that Dr. Nassar's right knee hurt him and this was due to rheumatic pains and it was not a dangerous thing.

Dr. Nassar was really complaining of some pains in his right knee and an operation in his knee was conducted for him before, in Germany, in September, 1996, and the doctor advised him to assemble an artificial knee. Then, Sai Baba told Dr. Nassar that he was a family man, reasonable, kind, satisfied, and happy.

Dr. Nassar told Sai Baba that he believed in spirituality since he was young and now, he was seventy six years old. At that time, Sai Baba said that He was seventy five years old and asked if He seemed so old. Dr. Nassar answered, saying that He seemed to be much younger than that and all of us laughed. Dr. Nassar told Him that he painted an oil portrait of Him, wishing Him to accept it. Sai Baba told him that He received it. Dr. Nassar told Him that he hoped that Swami would bless his book. Sai Baba put His hand on the book, saying He had blessed it.

Nefertiti talked to Him, asking Him to bless her children. He asked her, "How many kids did you have?" She answered, "Three kids." He said, "You wanted to beget a girl, but all your kids are boys. There is no difference between a girl and a boy. Both of them are Allah sons." Then, He pointed to her, saying, "I fulfilled your demand." Ani asked Him to bless his health and his family. Sai Baba said, "Yes, I did." He advised Ani to obey his father and mother, as he sometimes disobeyed them, saying that Father and Mother have a very respectable position. Ani asked Sai Baba to give him a souvenir. Swami smiled and stood up, after having finished speaking, in order to go out. Sai Baba put His right hand on Ani's head, then holding His hand, lead us to the external room. Then, He asked the Belgium wife and her husband to enter the internal room and He stayed with them for about ten minutes.

After that, they went out. He called the young man coming from Venezuela, to come in and He stayed with him for some minutes. Then, He came to us in the first room. He sat on the chair, while all of us were sitting on the floor, and He began to speak with us, saying,

"What is religion?"

"Religion is realisations."

"What is worry?"

"Worry is mental hesitation between good and bad."

He said that He was so much concerned about education, health, and water. As water was very important, there was no life without water. Thus, water is life.

"Look," He pointed at a big tableau on the floor beside the wall, on which a hospital was painted, "I had established a new hospital in Bengaluru for the highly accurate medical specialisation's tech, such as neurosurgery."

Dr. Nassar said that he visited the hospital, which was specialised in open heart operation, urinary passages, kidney transfer, and ophthalmology operation. The hospital was located in Puttaparthi and it was a very great hospital.

Sai Baba asked, "Where could the poor patient go, when he needed to be treated? The poor people should have the right for education and medical treatment for free and that is what we are doing."

Swami continued saying, "But, in Egypt, education and medical treatment is for gaining more money. Nothing for the poor people. There is no love in Egypt."

Then, He said, "In order to be so near God, you had to be characterised by purity, patience, and perseverance and you had to seek union with God." Then, He looked at Mrs. Randa, asking her whether she liked to wear like this robe, referring to the orange robe, which He was wearing. She was astonished and didn't answer him. But, Mrs. Laila replied quickly, "Yes, I like a robe." He smiled, went out of the room, going to another side room, and then, He returned to us with two robes, one of them for Mrs. Randa and the other for Mrs. Laila.

He asked them whether they were happy at that time. They answered in an affirmative form. Both of them took the robe in their arms. He asked them to put the robe under their heads, while sleeping, in order to dream of Sai Baba.

Then, He asked Mrs. Randa, "Where is your watch?" She was not wearing a watch in her left hand. She answered, "I forgot it in Egypt." At that time, we found a watch in her right hand. He ordered her to go to Him in order to put the watch on her left wrist, while we were so astonished as well as so happy. He said that it was a new model and it fitted her. The watch was metal. Mrs. Randa bowed before Him and kissed His hand. Then, Sai Baba asked who was going to travel the next day. Dr. Nassar answered him, saying that he and his family, Nefertiti and Ani, would travel the next day. Then, He looked to the rest of the group, asking them the same question. All of them answered, "After a week." Sai Baba smiled and said, "Fine."

Ani asked Sai Baba again, to give him a souvenir. He smiled and asked the Belgium woman to give Him the basket, which was on a shelf in the room. Then, He began to give us small bags, which contained the holy ash 'Vibhuti'. This ash contains a big spiritual energy. If a person puts a little of it in his mouth, his health would be improved and if one puts a little in any part, which hurt him, he would be better.

We went out after thanking Sai Baba, feeling so happy and comfortable, because of what we heard from Him. Most people in Puttaparthi knew that the Master met us in His private room (we knew that Thursday was the holy day for Sai Baba).

After having breakfast, I went to the library with Dr. Nassar to buy some books about Sai Baba and some books, which He wrote.

That these books were so great, valuable, and were so cheap to encourage people to read. We were keen to visit the museum the same day with Dr. Nassar, his son, and his daughter, who considered this day a historical, unforgettable day after meeting Sai Baba. We spent about three hours in the museum, but it needed much more time to know all the details concerning Sai Baba, His work, and His miracles. We entered the museum, not paying money as it was for free. The building was so luxurious and there was a developed technology in exhibiting.

We can see the Indian architectural art in its best form, colours, and statues. The showrooms were air-conditioned, organised, and so accurate. The museum was related to Sai Baba's life story, His miracles, and His discourses from the time He was a child up till now.

Also, there were books about the five religions, in which Sai Baba believed, which were Buddhism, Hinduism, Zoarashtranism, Christianity, and Islam.

About Islam, there was an embodied pattern of a mosque in Istanbul, as well as a golden pattern of the door of Kabba in Mecca.

After my visit to Puttaparthi and meeting Sai Baba, I believed that He was a great spiritual Master, Who had high spiritual potentialities and knew divine laws that helped Him to spread His humanitarian mission, which called for divine love, peace, good conduct, truth, and non-violence.

Sai Baba's name was Sathya, which means Truth. They called Him SRI, which meant Master, as well as Bhagawan, which meant Supreme Lord and Swami, which meant Holy. All these were names of Sai Baba. They consider Him a holy person by all means.

Any person, who had the opportunity to see Him, should raise his hand to greet Him as well as to bow before Him. If one was near Him, he should bow down and kiss His dress, as it was not allowed to touch His body.

I had seen the One, who called for divine love, goodness without discrimination because of religion, sex, or colour. The One, Who made miracles without seeking power, but for convincing people, saying that it was a visitng card. I had seen the Person, Who defended and took care of the poor. The Person, Who believed that everyone should have the right of education, medical treatment, and drinking water for free either in India, or outside it. All human beings were all equal for Him. I had seen the Person, Who was able to turn a poor, under developing area surrounded with hills and rocks, into a developed community, where there were schools and a university. The schools provided the young students with residence, food, education, and health care. In these schools, the student learnt academic sciences, as well as spirituality and human values, in order to become a good citizen. In addition, there was a big stadium for sports, artistic institutes, and museum, as Swami was concerned with sport and art, and its impact on the child.

I had seen a community full of security, love, and peace, in which poor and rich people all over the world were gathering, competing for voluntary work for serving others. If two persons met, we hear the word 'SAI RAM', which means peace. Everybody felt safe about himself and his personal properties.

I had seen the Person, Who applied the divine spiritual instructions inside India and outside it.

Many centres for Sai Baba were already established in many places all over the world, which called for His noble spiritual mission whether in USA or in Europe. Whenever you walked in the Ashram, you could see statements written in tableaus, such as:

Love is to give and forgive.
Selfishness is to get and forget.
If you lose wealth, you lost nothing.
If you lose health, you lost something.
If you lose character, you lost everything.
Duty is God and Work is Worship.

These above mentioned statements were some of His instructions to His followers, who learnt it by hearing and always work according to these instructions.

Now, was it possible to deny the existence of Allah? The way to be near Him was love and peace.

In the courtyard of Sai Baba's house, there was a big marble shaft. Its height is about 15 metres and its diagonal was one metre. On its top, there were flower leaves and its base had five sides. There were drawings on each side that represented one of the five religions. This shaft was established on the occasion of Sai Baba's Golden Birthday on 23rd November, 1975, which symbolised the unity of religions.

That was all about Sai Baba, the great spiritual Master. Our journey was really considered to be 'A JOURNEY TO SELF-PEACE'.

Dr. Abdelfattah M. Badawi

Symptoms Of Self-Peace

- A tendency to think and act spontaneously, rather than from fears based on past experiences.
- An unmistaken ability to enjoy each moment.
- A loss of interest in judging self.
- A loss of interest in judging others.
- A loss of interest in conflict.
- A loss of interest in interpreting the action of others.
- A loss of the ability to worry (This symptom is very serious).
- Frequent overwhelming episodes of appreciation.
- Contented feelings of connectedness with others and nature.
- Frequent attacks of smiling through the eyes of the Heart.
- Increasing susceptibility to love extended by others and the uncomfortable urge to extend it.
- An increasing tendency to let things happen, rather than make them happen.

If you have all or most of the above symptoms, please be advised that your condition of PEACE may be so far advanced as to not be treatable.

Bibliography

1. Burckhardt, Titus. An introduction to Sufi Doctrine. Great Britain: Thorsons Publishers Limited, 1976.

2. Cleveland, Ann. Truth is only one. Puttaparthi, India: Sai Publications, 1998.

3. Corbin, Henry. The Man of Light in Iranian Sufism. New York: Omega Publications Inc., 1971.

4. Danner, Mary Ann Koury. The Key to Salvation and the Lamp of Souls. UK: The Islamic Texts Society, 1996.

5. De Rola, Stanislas Klossowski. Alchemy. London: Thames and Hudson, 1973.

6. Kamath, M. and Kher, V., Sai Baba of Shirdi, a Unique Saint. Bombay, India: Jaico Publishing House, 1995.

7. Khan, Inayat. The Alchemy Of Happiness. Madras, India: Motilal Banarsidas, 1989.

8. Nasr, Seyyed Hossein. Living Sufism. Great Britain: Unwin Paperbacks, Mandala Books, 1972.

9. Pryor, Amineh Amelia. Psychology in Sufism. California: International Association of Sufism, 2000.

10. Rigopoulos, Antonio. The Life and Teachings of Sai Baba of Shirdi. Delhi, India: Sri Satguru Publications, 1993.

11. Sai Baba. Sathya Sai Speaks, Puttaparthi, India: Sai Publications (1953-1984).

12. Sai Baba: Dharma Vahini, Dhyana Vahini, Leela Vahini, Jnana Vahini, Prasanthi Nahini, Prema Vahini, Sathya Sai Vahini, Vidya Vahini, Sutra Vahini, Upanishad Vahini, Puttaparthi, India: Sai Publications (1999-2000).

13. Van Franz, Marie-Louise. Alchemical Active Imagination. Boston: Shambhala Publications Inc., 1997.

14. Warren, Marianne. Shirdi Sai Baba in the Light of Sufism. New Delhi, India: Sterling Publications, 1999.

www.ingramcontent.com/pod-product-compliance
Lightning Source LLC
Chambersburg PA
CBHW061325040426
42444CB00011B/2778